D. M. Matthews

Semi-centennial History of the Frenchtown M.E. Church

With a Chapter of Reminiscences, and brief Sketches of the Pastors

D. M. Matthews

Semi-centennial History of the Frenchtown M.E. Church
With a Chapter of Reminiscences, and brief Sketches of the Pastors

ISBN/EAN: 9783337209148

Printed in Europe, USA, Canada, Australia, Japan

Cover: Foto ©ninafisch / pixelio.de

More available books at **www.hansebooks.com**

Frenchtown M. E. Church.

OF THE

Frenchtown M. E. Church

WITH

A Chapter of Reminiscences,

AND

BRIEF SKETCHES OF THE PASTORS,

ALSO

A Chapter on the part this Church Bore in Suppressing the Rebellion

BY

D. M. MATTHEWS.

TRENTON, N. J.
FRANK SMITH, BOOK AND JOB PRINTER, 25 EAST STATE STREET
1895.

D. M. MATTHEWS.

CONTENTS.

CHAPTER I.

Early History of Asbury Circuit—1817-1832.

CHAPTER II.

Preliminary History Continued; Old Documents; Original Subscriptions; First Report of the Board of Trustees.

CHAPTER III.

Organization of the Frenchtown M. E. Church.

CHAPTER IV.

Reminiscences by John W. Lequear, Esq., Revs. A. M. Palmer, Walter Chamberlin, Cornelius Clark and Joseph Gaskill.

CHAPTER V.

Brief Personal Sketches of the Pastors who have Served the Frenchtown M. E. Church.

CHAPTER VI.

Brief Personal Sketches of the Pastors who have Served the Frenchtown M. E. Church—Continued.

CHAPTER VII.

The Part the Frenchtown M. E. Church Bore in Suppressing the Rebellion.

CHAPTER VIII.

Epworth League.

CHAPTER IX.

A Brief History of the Sunday School, with a List of Superintendents; A List of the Trustees of the Church from 1845 to 1895; Ladies' Aid Society with a List of Members.

CHAPTER X.

Semi-Centennial Exercises; Brief Outlines of Sermons; Subscription List for the Semi-Centennial Book.

PREFACE.

IN the preparation of this semi-centennial history, we have aimed at two things, viz: brevity and correctness. We have found it absolutely necessary to reduce the compass of our contributed articles.

We have laid under tribute the journal of Bishop Asbury, volume one, two and three, and the Minutes of the Annual Conference from 1817 to the present time.

In addition to the acknowledgements made in the volume where the articles are found, we are indebted to the manuscript of Rev. E. M. Griffith, deceased; Rev. John F. Dodd, D. D., Secretary of the Newark Conference; Will D. Nichols, for a drawing of the church, and N. J. Tomer and Rev. E. H. Conklin, for valuable assistance.

Acknowledging these aids we send it forth conscious of its many imperfections, but with the hope that, possibly, future writers in this line of work will here find a record of valuable facts that would otherwise have been lost. We trust our humble efforts may be of some interest to the church and to the community.   D. M. M.

FRENCHTOWN, N. J., December, 17th, 1895.

Published by and for the benefit of the trustees of Frenchtown M. E. Church.

The committee may in the near future prepare a supplementary volume, containing a roll of members of this church, with brief memoirs of the deceased.

CHAPTER I.

Cast thy bread upon the waters, for thou shalt find it after many days.—Eccl. XI 1.

THERE is much in the history of every church, said Edwin Warriner, "and in the life-story of each individual Christian to illustrate, and magnify the grace of God." But in writing this semi-centennial sketch it is not so much our purpose to magnify the present, or eulogize any individual, but to delve into the misty records of the past and leave the present for the future historian.

The first M. E. Church erected in this region was at Kingwood, in the year 1816 or '17, during the ministration of Rev. Manning Force. The circuit was called Asbury and the colleague of Rev. M. Force was George Banghart. The preacher in charge was much interested in the enterprise. Thomas West gave the lot, and was one of the original trustees. The preaching had been at his house previously. At that time Asbury circuit extended as far down as Trenton.

The preachers on the circuit afterwards were:

1817—George Banghart, R. W. Petherbridge.

1818—Sylvester G. Hill, James Aikins.

1819—Sylvester G. Hill, Waters Burrows.

1820—Waters Burrows, J. Creamer.

1821—John Creamer, Daniel Parish.

1822—William Leonard, James Moore.

1823—D. Bartine, Samuel Doughty.

1824—B. Collins, Samuel Doughty.

1825—B. Collins, Isaac Winner.

During the ministration of Rev. B. Collins, the Everittstown Church was erected.

1826—I. Winner, A. Atwood.

1827-'28—John Findley, J. K. Shaw. Each traveling the circuit two years.

1829—William A. Wiggins, G. Brown.

1830—William A. Wiggins, A. Gearhart.

1831—Pharaoh Ogden, Francis A. Morrell.

1832—James Long, Francis A. Morrell.

The Rev. F. A. Morrell favors E. M. Griffith with a list of preaching places on the circuit as they were when he traveled it.

"The circuit was about two hundred and fifty miles in a zigzag course around it. The Sabbath appointments were as follows: Asbury, ten A. M.; Bethlehem, over the mountains, three P. M. The former, an old church, an iron rod running through the building and fastened at both ends to keep the walls from parting. The latter, an unfinished edifice newly erected; Kingwood, ten A. M., in a good church. Preacher's home at Wilson Bray's; Everittstown, three P. M., in a new church unfinished. Put up at old Brother Everitt's; Lebanon, ten A. M. The church only enclosed, very cold in Winter, wind whistling through the knot holes. Stopping place, Jeremiah Huff's; Cokesbury, three P. M. The church had been erected some years previously but was not seated. The pulpit was the old carpenter's work bench, rather perilous to stand upon. Conrad Apgar's was the preacher's home; Washington, ten A. M. Stopping place Gershom Rusling's. The church was a small brick building; Thatcher's church, three P. M. This was a stone building and the wasps constituted the larger portion of the audience, often crawling on my neck and head. Put up at Thatcher's; Flander's, ten A. M. In a small church but large congregation. Put up at Judge Monroe's. This was a fine family, always giving the preachers a hearty welcome; Lawrence's barn, Millbrook, on the hill at three P. M. Stopped at Lawrence's; Dover, in the academy in the evening. Put up at a Brother Doty's."

As there is work for five Sabbaths marked down here, Rev. E. M. Griffith directed an inquiry to Brother Morrell concerning the fifth Sabbath. He explains as follows: "The circuit was divided at the close of my first year, I have given you two Sunday appointments not on the first year's plan, making as you suppose the fifth. The Sabbath appointments for the first year were: Asbury and Washington, in Warren; Kingwood and Everittstown, Lebanon and Cokesburg, in Hunterdon; Flanders, Millbrook and Dover, in Morris County. The week day appointments were numerous." As far as remembered by Brother Morrell they are here given.

"Joseph Smith's dwelling, Jugtown, near Asbury; Baptisttown in the evening, preached and put up at Brother Fox's; Bloomsbury occasionally: on the summit of a high mountain between Asbury and Bloomsbury, name forgotten; Stier's, in his own house in Hunterdon near Lebanon; Brother George Fisher's, in the woods; Tewksbury township, on Monday evenings; Tuesdays, rode ten miles to Thomas Walton's and John Fisher's alternately; about the roughest country I ever traveled through; preached at eleven A. M.; Thence, the next day

(Wednesday) to Squire Hagen's where I stopped, and preached in the school-house in the evening; thence, on the day following, Thursday, rode to Stanhope, preached in the school-house in the evening, put up with Brother McCormick. Sometimes on this evening preached at General Smith's at old Andover. On the morning of this day at eleven o'clock preached at old Mrs. Smith's on Schooley's Mountain, about four miles from Flanders; on Saturday preached in German Valley, in a school-house, I think. And on the following Monday evening at Peter Kemple's, Hackettstown. I think there were some other preaching places."

In the year 1833, Kingwood first appeared in the minutes as a separate charge, and Jacob Heavener was sent to travel it. The following year (1834) he was returned, and the minutes add "one to be supplied." In 1835, Abraham Gearhart and B. N. Reed were on the circuit. In 1836, Kingwood drops out of the appointments in the minutes. It was probably returned to Asbury circuit. A. Gearheart and R. Lanning were the preachers. It then took three weeks to travel the circuit reaching from Asbury and as far south as Sergeantsville. Abraham Slack's house was one of the first preaching places, dating back to about 1806. Elwood Servis now resides on the place, and it is known as Slacktown.

This year (1836), Flemington became the head of a somewhat extended circuit. It had previously been in the list of charges but was probably a station. The same year New Jersey was set off from the Philadelphia Conference and in the New Jersey Conference minutes Flemington stands with Jacob Heavener and J. M. Tuttle as the ministers to cultivate it. These brethren were returned to this field the next Spring, filing out two years on the circuit. In 1839, Wm. Hanley and J. White were the preachers. In 1840, A. K. Street and George Hitchens, traveled this circuit, and it was included in the Newark District with M. Force as Presiding Elder. In 1841, A. K. Street and Washington Thomas did the work. This year Flemington circuit was put into Newton District with Daniel Parish, Presiding Elder.

Asbury circuit, which as has been seen in the previous pages, covered the ground now included in Frenchtown charge was, (as has also been seen) very extensive. As late as 1832, as stated in F. A. Morrell's letter, its preaching places, commencing with Kingwood in the south reached to and included Dover in the north, and from Delaware to Washington. The Delaware proved an obstacle to labor further west for the bridges at Frenchtown and Milford did not exist. The Frenchtown bridge was erected in 1844; the Milford in 1841.

On the other side the Delaware, appointments were made by the

Northampton circuit preachers. Evidence of their presence as early as 1813 is afforded by a Bible at S. S. Shuster's, the property of his mother, a legacy from her father. The inscription on the fly leaf sets forth that the volume had been purchased by Henry Snyder—S. S. Shuster's grandfather—of Daniel Ashton, August 23d, 1813, price ten dollars. Henry Snyder then occupied the place, now owned by Wilson Lear, a half mile west of Erwinna. Here Ashton preached in the barn, but we have not been able to find out whether this was a regular or an occasional appointment. Tradition asserts that Rev. H. Boehm (a centenarian, who died December 28th, 1875), preached over in Pennsylvania in the Pursell neighborhood, below Bridgeton. The minutes of the Annual Conference inform us that H. Boehm was stationed on Chester circuit in 1824-'25. This date we thus fix upon as the possible date of his service there. After that time it seems to have fallen to the lot of the Asbury circuit preachers to give them such service as they could render.

At Milford an appointment we are inclined to think was early made. Rev. F. A. Morrell relates an interesting incident of his ministry when traveling Asbury circuit in 1832. He was expected to preach in the Pursell neighborhood. On reaching Milford the river was in a flood and he had difficulty in persuading the brother with whom he put up to venture, but finally he found a batteau and rowed him across. It was after all "love's labor lost." No one came to the place to hear him because nobody thought he could get across. Brother Pursell lectured him for the risk of his life, but Brother Morrell established a reputation for reliability thereby.

The church at Milford was erected at a much later period. It was dedicated in 1855 by Rev. Ryon, of Philadelphia.

Roll of pastors that have served the Frenchtown M. E. Church from the organization of the first class to the present time, are as follows:

Joseph Gaskill......................................1842
Z. Gaskill..1843
A. M. Palmer..1845-'46
T. T. Campfield . ...1847-'48
S. W. Decker...1849-'50
Rodney Winans and J. Horner...................1851-'52
Curtis Talley........ 1853
James Harris...1854
T. T. Campfield...1855-'56
William M. Burrows.....................................1857-'58

J. W. Barrett...1859
G. H. Jones..1860
W. Chamberlin   ....1861-'62
W. E. Blakeslee...1863-'64
H. J. Hayter.................... ....1865-'66 '67
J. B. Taylor..1868-'69-'70
Cornelius Clark, Jr.,............. ....1871-'72-'73
H. C. McBride.............................. 1874
E. M. Griffith......... 1875
E. M. Griffith and P. G. Ruckman...............1876
J. H. Runyon.................... . ...1877-'78-'79
T. E. Gordon ....1880-'81
I. N. Vansant...1882-'83-'84
S. D. Decker...1885-'86-'87
J. O. Winner, Sen............. ....1888-'89
M. T. Gibbs ....1890-'91
William McCain..1892-'93-'94
E. H. Conklin..... ....1895-'96

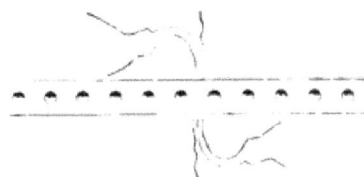

CHAPTER II.

PRELIMINARY HISTORY CONTINUED; OLD DOCUMENTS; ORIGINAL SUBSCRIPTIONS; FIRST REPORT OF THE BOARD OF TRUSTEES.

He that goeth forth and weepeth, bearing precious seed, shall doubtless come again with rejoicing, bringing his sheaves with him.—Psalms CXXVI-6.

WHEN Methodism was first introduced within the bounds of the present Borough of Frenchtown, it is impossible for the writer to state. It is a matter of history that Bishop Asbury traveled through Hunterdon County early in the present century.

In the year 1811, May 8th, quoting from his journal, page 308, volume three, "Crossed the Delaware River and sat down in Godley's school-room and taught the people; my subject was, Acts, third chapter, 26th verse." Again according to his journal we find him in the same year breaking the Bread of Life at the house of Thomas Pursell, who was an uncle of Mrs. Hannah Slack, of Frenchtown. The location of Pursell's was between Frenchtown and Milford, on the opposite side of the river a little south of the latter place. This was a preaching place for a quarter of a century. Bishop Asbury's death occurred March 21st, 1816. It is more than probable, however, that the introduction of Methodism in Frenchtown was by a local preacher, Rev. Amos Merselius, who was a member of the Kingwood M. E. Church, and a zealous worker for the Master's kingdom. He was at one time a politician of some note, and was appointed by the Legislature a Commissioner of Deeds for Kingwood township. The writer remembers hearing him preach in 1854. He died April 17th, 1870. Edward Hinkle remembers hearing Mr. Merselius preach a sermon in a house on Bridge street in 1832, and the first class of eleven members was formed in 1842, in John Walbert's wheelwright shop by Rev. Joseph Gaskill. The writer remembers attending service there fifty years ago. Mr. Walbert died February 20th, 1885, and at the time of his death was a member of the Frenchtown Presbyterian Church.

The only surviving members of this class of eleven, as far as can be ascertained, are Mrs. Hannah Slack and Martha Conner, of Frenchtown. Cyrenius A. Slack (the deceased husband of Mrs. Hannah Slack) was a shoemaker by trade and resided in a house on

Bridge street now owned by Mrs. Jane Able. Religious services were frequently held here and their house was the stopping place of the early itinerant.

In 1843 the little society resolved to build a church and a Board of Trustees was elected.

The following is a copy of the original document :

FRENCHTOWN, Hunterdon Co., N. J.

Agreeable to the public notice of at least ten days, the male members of the congregation attending upon the Methodist Episcopal ministry in this village assembled, this 15th day of July, 1844, at the house of Cyrenius A. Slack for the purpose of electing seven Trustees for the Methodist Episcopal Church of this place. Thereupon the following persons were duly elected, viz:—Cyrenius A. Slack, Lewis M. Prevost, Ambrose Silverthorn, John V. Hull, John Rodenbaugh, Charles Shuster and Sylvester R. Chamberlin.

Z. GASKILL, Chairman.

CYRENIUS A. SLACK, Secretary.

We, the undersigned Trustees, having taken the oath of office, do hereby certify that we have assumed and taken the name and title of "The Methodist Episcopal Church, of Frenchtown, N. J."

Witness our hands this fifteenth day of July, A. D., one thousand eight hundred and forty-four.

C. A. SLACK,
AMBROSE SILVERTHORN,
JOHN V. HULL,
SYLVESTER R. CHAMBERLIN,
JOHN RODENBAUGH,
LEWIS M. PREVOST,
CHARLES SHUSTER.

The following is a copy of the form of oath taken by the trustees :

" We do solemnly swear that we will perform the duties of trustees to the Methodist Episcopal Church in Frenchtown, Hunterdon County, State of New Jersey, to the best of our knowledge and abilities.

Witness our hand and seal, this fourth day of December, 1846."

Witness present,   SAMUEL F. HUFF.   [SEAL.]
L. M. PREVOST.

SAMUEL PITTENGER. [SEAL.]

" Personally appeared before me L. M. Prevost, one of the Judges of the Inferior Courts of Common Pleas of Hunterdon County, State of

New Jersey, Samuel F. Huff and Samuel Pittenger, who after having
been informed by me of the contents of the above documents, did
severally subscribe to the same, and each took his oath before me as
required by law."

Witness my hand and seal, this fourth day of December, in the year
of our Lord 1846.   L. M. PREVOST.   [SEAL.]

One of the Judges of the Inferior Court of Common Pleas for County
of Hunterdon.

The above may be found on record at the Clerk's office in Flemington, N. J., Volume two, of special deeds for County of Hunterdon,
page 426.   BESSON, Clerk.

The lot on which the church stands was purchased of Hugh Capner;
price, one hundred dollars in specie, and the church was raised October 24th, 1844. We ascertained this fact from the fly leaf of Henry
Snyder's old Bible, now in possession of Joseph Ashton, of Trenton,
N. J. It will be seen by the following letter from Rev. A. M. Palmer
that the church was in an unfinished condition, and not formally dedicated until more than a year from the above date:

NEWARK, N. J., June 9th, 1894.

D. M. MATTHEWS.

DEAR BRO.:—Received to-day a copy of the *Independent* containing
your history of the Frenchtown Church. Under the ministry of
Brother Z. Gaskill, in the autumn of 1844 the building was enclosed,
floors laid, windows put in, etc. Temporary seats were made, much
like the seats of a primitive camp meeting, simply rough boards placed
on benches, and a stove was secured.

Brother Gaskill preached every other Sabbath in the afternoon, in
the unfinished building. There certainly could not have been any
dedicatory services at that time. In the Spring of 1845 I was appointed
to Quakertown circuit. And the house you name was secured for the
parsonage.

I was the first Methodist minister to reside in Frenchtown.

During the summer and autumn strenuous efforts were made to
finish the building. It was no easy thing to do, for the want of means.
I called on most everybody in the circuit interested in our church, and
then sent a man abroad to collect money for us.

During the early fall we had a gracious revival of religion. Finally
we felt that we were justified in proceeding to complete the building in
a plain way. It was completed and dedicated on Wednesday, December 17th, 1846.

Rev. Isaac Winner, then the Presiding Elder, preached in the morning. Rev. Abraham Owen, then stationed at New Germantown, preached in the evening. In my diary from which I take the above I find this: "services well attended and very interesting."

Yours truly,

A. M. PALMER.

Alfred R. Taylor and William Logan were the carpenters.

The following is the call for the erection of the church with the original subscription:

"WHEREAS, The inhabitants of Frenchtown and vicinity are destitute of a suitable place in which to worship Almighty God, and being desirous of a place of religious worship in said village, and whereas, the members and friends of the Methodist Episcopal Church contemplate erecting a house of worship in said village: We, whose names are hereto subscribed, agree to give the sum annexed to our names to aid in the erection of said house to be under the government of said church, according to the form laid down in the book of discipline of said church. The money to be paid to the trustees who may be duly appointed. To be given in installments as follows: One-third to be paid the first day of November, 1844, following. The residue on the first day of April, 1845."

John H. Prevost	$5 00
Wholston Vanderbelt	1 00
John T. Hull	20 00
William F. Moore	3 00
Isaac Johnston	5 00
S. C. Eckel	5 00
I. W. Housel	1 00
George Carpenter	1 00
Samuel Warne	2 00
Levi Case	1 00
Andrew Risler	1 00
Wesley Shuster	5 00
Joseph Johnson	2 00
Charles T. Fulper	1 00
Amos Opdycke	5 00
Jesse R. Huff	1 00
Jeremiah Matthews	3 00
Abraham Bennett	3 00
William Sarch	1 00
William Vanderbelt	1 00

Mordeica Thomas............... .... 1 00
T. and L. Vansyckel.. 1 00
John Matthews... 3 00

The original subscription was started at the wedding of John J.
Zane and Anna M. Williams. They were married at the old Williams
mansion, situated on the west bank of the Delaware, in Tinicum township, between Uhlertown and Lodi. The wedding took place February
22d, 1844, Z. Gaskill officiating.

The following names are not found on the old subscription as copied
above, but there is evidently a page or more lost. We add the seven
names on the authority of one who was there:

John M. Pursell $25 00
Mary Williams...... .... 25 00
Barzila Williams........ .. .. 10 00
T. Elwood Williams....................... 3 00
Anna Zane.. 2 00
J. J. Zane.. 2 00
Margaret Williams... .... 2 00

The following is a correct copy of the original subscription taken at
the dedication bearing date, December, 17th, 1845:

John V. Hull..$10 00
Ambrose Silverthorn........................... 10 00
Henry Snyder...................................... 10 00
Isaac Hartpence................................' 10 00
Samuel Vansyckle................................ 10 00
David Rockafellow........................ ..... 10 00
John Sipes... 5 00
William Roberson............................... 5 00
Thomas Roberson 5 00
Elizabeth Fox...... .... 5 00
Thomas Roberson, Jr................... 5 00
Horatio Opdyke................................ 5 00
Cyrenius A. Slack 5 00
Jeremiah Matthews........................... 5 00
Catharine Rittenhouse....................... 5 00
Joseph Everitt.................... .... 5 00
B. M. Pearsell........................:......... 5 00
Rachel West.. 5 00
Aaron Huffman.................................. 5 00
Lucy Roberson................................... 2 00
William Silverthorn.......................... 2 00
Zebulon Bodine...... .... 2 00

Isabella Vansyckle	2 00
Jesse R. Huff	2 00
John Snyder	2 00
John W. Fox	2 00
Stephen Hull	2 00
Jacob Rounseville	2 00
Ralph Tenyck	2 00
Adam Kitchen	2 00
Catharine Opdyke	2 00
William Leonard	2 00
William Moore	2 00
Ann Eliza Williams	2 00
Jane Silverthorn	2 00
N. D. Williams	1 00
Amos Hyde	1 00
Charles Roberson	1 00
Wesley Shuster	1 00
Mahlon Rittenhouse	1 00
Maria Creathers	1 00
Susan Case	1 00
Margaret Mettler	1 00
Elizabeth Thatcher	1 00
Mrs. Rockafellow	1 00
Rebecca Leonard	1 00
Sophia Hull	1 00
Esther Hull	1 00
Mary Ann Stout	1 00
William Jones	1 00
Solomon Stout	1 00
Frederick Apgar	1 00
Silvanas Runyon	1 00
M. W. Burger	1 00
Thomas Pittenger	50
William Besson	50
S. B. Hudnit	50
C. S.	1 00
William V. Sloan	5 00

The old parsonage was purchased of S. B. Hudnit for $850. The writer finds the following among Brother Obadiah Stout's papers.

"We, the undersigned, promise to pay the sums annexed to our names to the Trustees of the Methodist Episcopal Church, of Frenchtown, N. J., for the purpose of purchasing a parsonage for the use of said church.   Hereunto, we set our hands this 13th day of June, A D., 1853."

Henry Snyder	$20 00
Charles Green	15 00
S. B. Hudnit	15 00
Obadiah Stout	15 00
Richard Stockton	15 00
Joseph Ashton	15 00
Ozias P. Thatcher	15 00
Ralph Ten Eyck	10 00
Abner Salter	10 00
John Williams	5 00
Soloman Stout	10 00
Samuel Dalrymple	5 00
Mary Whiting	3 00

This subscription is mutilated and incomplete.

The original trustees have all left the Church Militant and gone we trust to join the Church Triumphant.   Charles Shuster was a German, and came from near the French border between the Moselle and the Rhine, landing at Philadelphia, July 21st, 1818.   He died October 20th, 1847, and is buried in the old grave-yard at Everittstown.

Sylvester R. Chamberlin was an undertaker and cabinet-maker, and lived where Benjamin Philkill now resides.   He died while comparatively a young man, November 8th, 1847, aged twenty-eight years.

The next to fall was John Rodenbaugh, who died near Frenchtown, February 26th, 1850.   He lived on the John Apgar farm.

Lewis M. Prevost followed, November 15th, 1872.   The family was of French origin, and during the French Revolution escaped into Germany and came to America about the commencement of the present century.   The family were large land-holders.   Lewis M. Prevost kept store in Frenchtown a number of years, and lived where Mayor Sherman now resides.   He was also Justice of the Peace and one of the Judges of the Court of Common Pleas.

Cyrenius A. Slack (late husband of Mrs. Hannah Slack, who resides on the corner of Third and Harrison streets) was the next to leave the shores of time.   He died December 31st, 1876.

Ambrose Silverthorn lived in the house now owned by Wilbur Slack, situated on the corner of Second and Harrison streets, where William Hoffman now resides.

Previous to this he was at the Frenchtown bridge for a number of years.   Levi Mettler was his successor.   Mr. Silverthorn removed to

Kansas and was killed by a runaway team of horses, November 24th, 1882.

John V. Hull, the last of the original trustees moved to Lambertville, where he died January 18th, 1891.

We close this chapter with the first report of the Board of Trustees, dating back fifty years.

C. A. SLACK IN ACCOUNT WITH M. E. CHURCH.

DR.

To cash from

	George Carpenter	$1	00
	John Rodenbaugh	5	00
	Rachel Silverthorn	2	00
1844.			
Sept.	Henry Snyder	20	00
	John V. Hull	5	00
Oct. 2.	Lime	2	50
26.	John Rodenbaugh	1	75
Nov. 9.	Ann Eliza Williams	5	00
9.	Mary Williams	8	00
29.	Mary Smity	5	00
	Barzila Williams	2	00
1845.			
March	Isaac Hartpence	3	00
April 7.	Hiram A. Williams	15	00
	Jonas Smith	3	00
	Barzila Williams	3	00
	Caroline Williams	1	00
	Amos Opdyke	5	00
April 17	Catharine Leonard	5	00
	George W. Waterhouse	1	00
	Joseph A. Halden	5	00
	John H. Prevost	5	00
	George Salter	1	50
May 3.	John V. Hull	4	11
	A. Silverthorn	6	12
May 5.	Jeremiah Matthews	3	00
	James Williams	15	00
	Mary Williams	17	00
	John Williams	5	00
	N. Williams	5	00
	Margaret Williams	1	00

	By C. Shuster	7	00
May 7.	A. Silverthorn	5	62
9.	Wilson Bray	5	00
	Andrew Williamson	5	00
	William Search	5	00
12.	Rachel Silverthorn	2	00
18.	By C. Shuster	3	00
24.	Thomas Silverthorn	2	00
27.	Hiram Bennett	2	00
June 2.	J. M. Pursal	25	00
July 6.	A. Silverthorn	1	75
27.	J. J. Zanes	2	00
	By a friend	3	00
	Daniel S. Pursal	1	00
	A. M. Palmer	5	00
	Jonas Thatcher		78
	C. Snyder		31
Jan. 31.	Jacob Fullmer	300	00
May	A. M. Palmer	8	00
	William F. Moore	110	00
	Error in Geo. Thorne's Act	1	00
	Ann E. Williams	2	00

CR.

By cash paid in book.

Sept. 3.	H. Capner's note	20	00
10.		18	00
17.	For nails		25
Oct. 2.	For lime	2	50
26.	William S. Jones	1	75
Nov. 13.	William Logan	1	00
14.	H. Capner's note	7	00
18.	For nails	1	70
	N. Williams	7	07
Dec. 30.	For nails		50
1845.			
Jan. 2.	Whitelead		55
7.	For nails	1	00
22.	For zink		30
April 7.	Hedges & Reading	25	00
22.	William Lippincott	11	00
	Hiram Deats	11	00

	Pittenger Fitzer	3	25
May 7.	John Case	57	00
		5	62
9.	L. M. Prevost	15	00
4.	Daniel Brink	8	55
27.	Hedges & Reading	10	00
June 2.		25	00
July 9.	For nails		80
Oct. 31.	For boards	1	98
	William S. Jones	3	00
13.	Expenses to Court	1	00
1846.			
Jan. 9.	Whiting & Cooley	1	98
	L. M. Prevost & Son	1	30
	William S. Jones	4	16
		75	

Receipts not in book.

Jan. 31.	L. M Prevost	50	00
	Hedges & Reading	50	00
	William Silverthorn	6	19
	William Huffman	20	00
	John Case	77	03
	William S. Jones	20	00
Feb. 4.	George Thorn	10	00
17.	John Sailor	1	11
24.	T. Pittenger	6	92
March 7.	S. C. Allen	1	62
14.	Insurance	17	70
23.	Hedges & Reading	24	16
April 18.	George Thorn	5	87
	William Huffmar	20	00
	John George	15	00
May 23.	" " in full	25	00
1.	William S. Jones	30	60
5.	Vansyckle	12	00
June 15.	Hiram Deats	9	72
July 31.	Whiting & Cooley	5	00
	" "	18	00
1845.			
Dec. 19.	A. M. Palmer	50	00

CHAPTER III.

ORGANIZATION OF THE FRENCHTOWN M. E. CHURCH.

So shall my words be that goeth forth out of my mouth: it shall not return unto me void, but it shall accomplish that which I please, and it shall prosper in the thing whereto I sent it — Isa. 55: 11.

WE copy the following, with some additions, from an article prepared by the writer, and read by Miss Laura Woolverton, before the Hunterdon County Historical Society at Frenchtown, N. J., June 22d, 1894:

The first step towards the organization of a Methodist Episcopal Church, is the formation of a class. It may consist of eight or twelve persons, with one appointed as leader. This is the door to membership in the church. Any person professing a desire to flee from the wrath to come and giving his or her name to the leader, after attending the meeting for six months, is eligible to membership in the church, by the recommendation of the leader. This first step toward the organization of the Frenchtown M. E. Church was taken in the year 1842, under the leadership of the Rev. Joseph Gaskill, who formed a classs of eleven persons. The following pastors have served the church in the order named. In speaking of them we will use brevity, because a personal sketch of the twenty-eight pastors will appear in another chapter.

The second on the list is Zerubbabel Gaskill, who was the pioneer temperance advocate in this field of labor. We are indebted to Rev. A. E. Ballard for the following, which is taken from the " New Jersey Conference Memorial :"

" He found the Quakertown circuit in a condition so deplorable that there were scarcely enough living to bury the dead. Bacchus, that fell demon of discord, said in his heart; I will ascent into heaven; I will exalt my throne above the stars of God; I will also sit upon the mount of the congregation in the sides of the north; I will ascend above the heights of the clouds; I will be like the Most High. Isaiah 14: 13-14. And he did get the upper hand of many of the stars of the congregation and also the leading men of the place. For these men discarded minister and church and God, all at the bidding of Bacchus. Mr. Gaskill prudently but fearlessly opened the batteries of truth against this citadel of satan. Men are always extremely sensitive when conscience is silenced at the demands of interest or self-indulgence. This was the case now, and the opposition becoming very formidable, first tried raising a storm of popular indignation to silence the stupid one-idea fanatic who was capable of the senseless temerity of insisting that Christians ought not to make, sell or drink rum ; and they did succeed in awaking the elements. The rains descended, the floods came and the winds blew ; but like the sturdy oak he only bent to the blast till its fierceness was spent and then stood up as firmly and defiant as before. Failing in this they changed their tactics and raised the cry of persecution, and if their version had been reliable it would have been true, that they were the most thoroughly abused of men. Failing also in this, and finding that neither weeds nor tufts of grass would do, they tried the virtue of stones. Two trustees of the church at Everitts-town, demanded the keys of the sexton and closed the house against him. But Amos Opdyke another of the trustees backed by others and aided by Wesley Johnson, a Presbyterian, who made a key, opened it for him to preach on the subject in question. Being foiled again a mob took the matter in hand and tried the persuasive powers of rotten eggs and other missiles, together with bonfires and yelling, and whooping like a pack of savages. Fortunately for the ministers and the cause, the ladies of some of the malcontents attended this service and received in part, the application of the egg argument. Meanwhile the appeal of the speaker was so calm, logical and convincing as to enlist the favor of the better part of the people and thus to secure a triumph. The turbulent party then threatened to waylay and lynch him if he attempted to fill an appointment at another place ; but he did meet the engage-ment and that, too, without being maltreated. These expedients failing they next resorted to the desperate alternative of an attempt to starve him out. When told of this design he replied, 'they might as well try to starve a bear.' Nor was this a vain boast. The sum he received cannot be named, but he was drven to perplexing straits. Friends aided him. He exchanged wheat flour for indian meal, because it would go further. He sold part of their scanty furniture and thus purchased the needed supplies for his family. At the same time he stood up to his convictions with manly and unflinching firmness, until the end of his term."

A. M. Palmer was his successor during 1845-'46. The house of Wilbur Slack, on the corner of Second street where Mr. Hoffman now

resides was then the parsonage. Brother Palmer now lives in Newark,
N. J., and is Conference Treasurer of the various benevolences of the
church. During his pastorate an episode occurred at a baptismal
service which took place a little below the bridge that spans the river.
David O. Roberson informs the writer that there were about fifty
baptisms and four of this number by immersion. Mary A. Fisher,
who afterwards became Mrs. David O. Roberson, Amy T. Pittenger
and Ann Calvin were three of the number. A young man hailing
from the rural district of Everittstown, by the name of Apgar thought
he would baptize a dog. Apgar climbed out on the root of a tree that
extended over the water with the dog in his arms, and when Brother
Palmer was about to immerse a subject in the name of the Holy
Trinity, said Apgar undertook to plunge the dog, but losing his footing
the dog and he both went in together and the latter came near drowning.

T. T. Campfield followed in 1847-'48; he also served another term,
1855-'56. During his second term as pastor the parsonage was
purchased.

S. W. Decker followed in 1849, and remained two years which was
then the time limit. He was something of a politician of the Demo-
cratic persuasion, and was elected Superintendent of public schools of
Alexandria township, which at that time included Holland township
and the Borough of Frenchtown. Brother Decker was the first
Methodist preacher in the remembrance of the writer to bring notes or
manuscript into the pulpit. It was considered at that time next to the
unpardonable sin and under no circumstances could be allowed. He
was waited upon by the church officials and requested to reform or
vacate the pulpit. At the close of his term he entered the New Jersey
State Prison as Chaplain.

In 1851-52 we find Rodney Winans with Joseph Horner in charge.
The circuit at that time took in Quakertown, Frenchtown, Milford,
Little York and Everittstown. They were both acceptable preachers,
above the average in pulpit efforts. There was a gracious revival at
Everittstown.

In 1853 Curtis Talley was pastor. This was his last charge.

In 1854 Brother Harris was the preacher in charge. He came from
the South and returned thither at the close of the year. In 1855-'56 T.
T. Campfield served a second term.

In 1857-'58 William M. Burrows' name appears. He served the
church acceptably for two years.

In 1859 J. W. Barrett was preacher in charge. The writer remembers
one sermon of his to this day from the text, Matthew, fourth chapter,
3d verse. He now resides in Newark, N. J.

George H. Jones followed him in 1860. He was an M. D., and in later years practiced medicine at Boonton and Phillipsburg. He was a prominent mason and a charter member of Orion Lodge, No. 56, F. and A. M. and the first W. M. of the same. He was also prominent in Oddfellowship and now resides in Camden, N. J.

Walter Chamberlin comes next in order, who served the church during 1861-'62, and now resides at Derby, Conn. The church at this time was greatly improved. A basement was put under, the side galleries were taken down, a spire erected and a bell purchased. The improved church was reopened February 28th, 1862, Bishop E. S. Janes officiating in the morning and Dr. Wiley in the evening. An amusing episode is remembered during his pastorate. Brother Chamberlin was an indefatigable laborer and very persistent in his way. An extra meeting had been in progress a number of weeks with but little apparent success. Near the close of the evening service he asked for an expression from the members if the meetings should be continued another week. The vote was in the negative. About that time a dog came perambulating up the aisle into the altar, but the animal's movements were greatly accelerated by the up-lifted foot of the pastor, while the dog hastened toward the door singing a tune to the key of a screechy G, while the dominie remarked, "The devil and the dogs always assemble with the people of God."

W. E. Blakeslee came in 1863, remaining two years. He is now filling one of the best appointments in the district—Fulton street, Elizabeth, N. J.

Henry J. Hayter was his successor. During his ministration the little barn in the rear of the church was built. He lives at Bradley Beach, N. J.

J. B. Taylor was pastor for the next three years, 1868-'70. The church was again enlarged, twenty feet being added to the rear, which accounts for its being all long and no wide. Brother Obadiah Stout was the contractor and did the work. At the second reopening O. H. Tiffany preached the first sermon, and in the evening Dr. John Hanlon officiated. This last sermon is remembered to this day for its eloquence and adaption. Brother Taylor is now stationed at Nyack, New York.

During 1871-'72 and '73, Cornelius Clark was in charge of the work. He was known as a progressive temperance champion. He founded and published a paper in the interest of prohibition called *The Home Visitor*, which now, if the writer is correctly informed, has the largest circulation of any local paper published in Hunterdon County. Brother Clark is at Rockaway, N. J.

H. C. McBride was here in 1874. He had conscientious scruples in regard to preaching in a pewed church. The seats were by order of the trustees made free and have remained so since.

He was followed by E. M. Griffith, P. G. Ruckman and J. H. Runyon, who served in the order named.

During the pastorate of the last named, the parsonage debt was paid.

E. M. Griffith's health failed during his second year on the charge. A committee appointed by the quarterly conference, offered the following resolutions which were unanimously passed:

Resolved, That we tender to the Rev. E. M. Griffith and family our heartfelt sympathy in this their affliction, and while in the providence of God he may no longer go in and out before this congregation as pastor, wherever his lot may fall, he and his family shall have a large place in our affections and prayers.

Resolved, That while it is with profound sorrow, we feel the necessity laid upon us of accepting his resignation, that we commit our cause to Him who is " too wise to err and too good to be unkind."

Resolved, That we hereby pledge ourselves to renewed diligence in the Master's cause, resolving in the strength of God's Eternal Son, though the workman fall the work shall not cease.

> D. M. MATTHEWS,
 A. S. HARRING,   *Committee.*
 S. D. SLACK.

After the failure of Brother Griffith's health, P. G. Ruckman filled the balance of the year, closing up with a gracious revival. He was afterwards a transfer to Nebraska where he remained seven years.

Thomas E. Gordon followed in 1880-'81 and was succeeded by I. N. Vansant, who remained three years. During the term of the latter the church was frescoed and beautified at an outlay of $1,000, all of which was provided for, and there was an aggressive movement in every department of Christian work. He is now pastor of the Bloomsbury M. E. Church.

S. D. Decker came in 1885, remaining three years, which were crowded with activities. The old parsonage was moved back, the present structure erected during his second year. During his last year the church was painted, at a cost of $215. He is stationed at Deckertown, Sussex County, N. J.

In 1888-'89 J. O. Winner was preacher in charge. His two years were years of seed-sowing and productive of good results.

1890-'91 M. T. Gibbs was pastor. During his first year the church was blessed with a revival of religion such as had never been seen in Frenchtown. He also organized an Epworth League which has been, and is a power for good. A committee was also appointed during his pastorate, consisting of L. D. Hagaman, Benjamin Philkill and the writer, to raise money to cancel a debt of $1,500, the most of which had been hanging over the society for a quarter of a century.

In 1892, William McCain became pastor and remained for three years. During his second year a Junior Epworth League was formed from which may come results as far reaching as Eternity. His three years here were characterized by the working of the Holy Spirit.

This was manifested most clearly internally in Christian experience. During the last year this inner light developed in a class-meeting revival, which was truly refreshing.

Difficult places were always made easy by the presence of God as a very present help in time of trouble. The congregations and mid-week meetings were good. During his second year there was a conflagration in the church; the fire broke out on a lovely Sabbath morning in May; one of the members of the present Board of Trustees is the guilty party. However, we are glad to chronical the church was not burned, but the last dollar of the evidence of indebtedness went up in smoke.

In 1895, the present pastor E. H. Conklin, was sent to Frenchtown. The barn was removed and sheds in the rear of the church erected during his first year, and in this, our semi-centennial, we are expecting an advance movement in every department of Christian work.

The following subscription lifted the last dollar of indebtedness :

William H. Rittenhouse	2 00
Edward Hinkle	15 00
W. H. Martin	10 00
Obediah Stout	3 00
Isaac T. Cronce	4 50
Hugh Echlin	13 00
Mrs. Solomon Stout	15 00
Mrs. K. Lancaster	1 50
Mary Pinkerton	3 00
Joseph Pickle and John O. Smith	130 00
Margaret Smith	2 00
D. M. Matthews	77 00
A. W. Lundy	10 00
Benjamin Philkill	15 00
Amy W. Anderson	3 00
Susan Johnson	50

Sarah J. Stout	1 00
Kate F. Henarie	25 00
David Roberson	75 00
Mary Hummer	1 00
William C. Kline	8 00
John H. Kline	20 00
Judson Hoff	1 00
James E. Sherman	15 00
Sedgwick Gano	1 50
Samuel Gano	2 00
Priscilla Hartpence	4 50
Mrs. Andrew Slack	5 00
N. T. Rittenhouse	25 00
Catherine A. Wanamaker	10 00
William B. Horner	1 00
Reuben K. Niece	45 00
William Silverthorn	12 00
B. F. Fisher	2 00
Ella Shurtz	40 00
Joseph Aller	10 00
George Stinsman	5 00
Mindy Britton	2 00
Mrs. Wright	1 00
John W. Pinkerton	3 00
Margaret Roberson	3 00
Rebecca Kimble	6 00
James Kugler	3 00
Slack & Holcombe	10 00
Henry Cronce and wife	1 00
Mrs. Loraine Opdyke	1 25
Wilson Roberson	3 00
Fayette Burgstresser	2 50
G. Lambert Everitt	1 00
Mrs. Opdyke	1 00
Lavina Pittinger	3 00
Lizzie Rittenhouse	1 00
N. R. Sinclair	1 00
Mona H. McClain	1 00
Sylvester B. Horner	2 00
Porter Tettermer	5 00
Mrs. Daniel M. Everitt	4 00
Lucretia Roberson	1 00

Harry Grover	10 00
Albert Sinclair	3 00
Mrs. Sarah Horner	1 00
L. S. D. Kerr	50 00
Hezekiah Hoff	15 00
Mrs. Elizabeth Wright	2 00
H. B. Hawk	10 00
S. S. Shuster	10 00
N. R. Shuster	5 00
L. D. Riegel	1 00
Judson Kugler	3 00
T. W. Holcombe	10 00
W. H. Sipes	1 50
G. W. Hummer	45 00
W. H. Stahler	11 00
Levi Case & Son	35 00
Harriet Barcroft	30 00
W. V. Gordon	3 00
Ann Scuyler	1 00
F. W. Opdyke	5 00
Alfred Curtis	5 00
Miss Lizzie Smith	5 00
Samuel M. Rittenhouse	1 00
Mrs. George Snyder	1 00
Kate Rittenhouse	5 00
Harry S. Slack	1 00
S. H. Stahler	1 00
Peter Stryker	1 00
Charles B. Salter	1 00
D. D. Britton	1 00
Tillie Trimmer	50
Mrs. Annastatia A. Warford	1 00
M. E. Srope	2 00
A. H. Vreeland	5 00
Sylvester Riegel	4 00
Peter A. Fisher and wife	4 00
Wilbur Slack	20 00
L. D. Hagaman and wife	75 00
Samuel Dalrymple	5 50
H. W. Bellis	3 00
Chester Taylor	1 00
Alonzo Butler	2 00

John R. Apgar	1 00
Mrs. Morris Maxwell	5 00
Wm. P. Loper	1 00
Andrew Slack	20 00
Samuel Opdyke	1 00
Rev. Wm. H. McCain	25 00
Hannah Williams	5 00
E. W. Bloom	45 00
Edward Rittenhouse	30 00
Edward Lair	12 00
Wm. Gorden & Son	45 00
Theo. Fritts	3 00
John L. Slack	15 00
Morris Maxwell	5 00
L. M. Hoffman	30 00
Josiah Butler	4 00
John P. Lance	2 00
Mrs. Daniel Stahler	2 00
Augustus Cronce	3 00
Lucy Snyder	2 00
Belle M. Webster	1 00
Matilda Nixon	1 00
Sarah Sinclair	1 00
Kate Taylor	2 00
Mrs. Leidy	3 00
Anna A. Lyons	3 00
Rev. M. T. Gibbs	10 00
W. Blakeslee and mother	2 25
Sophia T. Hoff	7 00
Mrs. Irving McClain	3 00
I. L. Niece	30 00
Mary C. Swan	2 00
F. B. Fargo	75 00
Ura Larue	2 00
Phœbe V. Stryker	1 75
Matilda J. Risler	1 50
Frank F. Maxwell	3 00
A. P. Williams	1 00
Mary Cronce	1 00
Mrs. S. L. Reading	12 50
Wm. Niece and wife	17 50
George F. Bloom	7 00

Thomas Mechling.............................. 2 00
Mary McClain...................................... 2 00
Mrs. Houghawout.............................. 1 00
Charles R. Everitt and wife............... 4 00
Wm. E. Culver.................................... 1 00

3 *

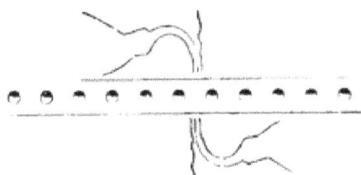

CHAPTER IV.

Reminiscences by John W. Lequear, Esq., Revs. A. M. Palmer, Walter Chamberlin, Cornelius Clark and Joseph Gaskill.

> " 'Tis greatly wise, to talk with our past hours,
> And ask them what report they bore to Heaven,
> And how they might have borne more welcome news."

Reminiscences by J. W. Lequear.

IN contemplating the change time has wrought even in this county, one is filled with surprise and thankfulness. At my birth there was not a single newspaper published in this county, and now there are not less than a dozen. The first one published was the *Hunterdon Gazette and Farmers' Weekly Advertiser*, by Charles George, March 24, 1825. Churches were few. There were none in Milford, Frenchtown, Stockton, and only one in Lambertville — the Presbyterian Church —built, I think, in 1818; indeed, but few houses in any of these villages. St. Thomas Stone Episcopal Church, near the northern boundery of Kingwood, and the St. Andrew Episcopal Church, at Ringoes, and the old stone Presbyterian Church.

The Baptists occupied much of the intervening country, and wherever they settled they gave a free opportunity to all others to settle and enjoy their religious belief without fear or molestation. Their place of meeting was at Baptisttown, with occasional preaching at outlying stations. There was not a single Methodist Church in the county.

About the year 1815, the Methodists formed a class and began to hold meetings in Kingwood at the house of Thomas West. In the year 1816 they purchased a lot from Mr. West's farm, and soon set about building the first Methodist house of worship in the county, so far as I know. Before the building of their house, they held out-door meetings in Mr. West's woods; a large rock still bears the name of Pulpit Rock. The first trustees were: Thomas West, Joseph West, Jacob Hart, Darius Everitt, Christopher Snyder, William Serch, and Abraham Slack, some of whom were well known to the writer.

Soon after this they held a camp meeting below Milltown, near William Keer's present residence. I cannot obtain the names of the preachers who took part in this meeting, but presume Manning Force, then a young preacher, took an active part in it, as he was instrumental in organizing this society. The first preachers I remember hearing were Manning Force and Jacob Heavener. Mr. Force was a tall, slender man, of fine, pleasant countenance and sweet-toned voice, while Mr. Heavener was an energetic speaker full of zeal in his fiery denunciations of sin.

The Fox Hill Methodist Society was organized, I think, about the year 1819. After some years Manning Force became presiding elder. The distance from Fairmount to Kingwood is about thirty miles. I frequently saw Mr. Force making the journey on horseback, with his saddle-bags strapped on behind, containing his clothes, and oftentimes the mud was nearly knee deep, requiring him to wear overalls to protect him from the mud. This good man died February 22, 1862, aged seventy-two years, having passed fifty-one years in the ministry.

The Bray family emigrated from Middletown, Monmouth County, in 1713, purchasing land and settling in Kingwood. They were earnest Baptists in their religious faith. The West family were members of the first Methodist class formed in Kingwood. Wilson Bray having married Mary West, he united soon after with the Methodists. Two years after his term as Sheriff had expired, he bought the homestead and farm of his father-in-law, Thomas West, who resided near the Kingwood M. E. Church, to which he removed from Flemington. They had a large family of sons and daughters, and this home became the " Preacher's Home " until Mr. Bray's death. The itinerant preachers always felt sure of a social and Christian welcome.

I think it was in the fall of 1838 that the great revival took place in this church, conducted by Rev. James M. Tuttle. I remember being there the first night he preached, and remember his text : " Behold, I stand at the door and knock." This earnest servant of God died November 22, 1887, aged seventy-eight years, after fifty-one years in the ministry.

I have a distinct remembrance of hearing many of the old-time ministers, but have forgotten their names ; perhaps Caleb Lippencot was one of the first I became acquainted with, preaching at Kingwood and Sergeantsville in 1845 ; he was a portly man, a plain, but earnest speaker. But the first preacher I became intimately acquainted with was Stacy W. Hilliard, who was about my own age, and we became warm friends. He died August 31st, 1873.

Soon after the erection of the Frenchtown Church, but in an unfinished state, I attended a class-meeting conducted by Henry Eisenbry, of Lumberville. I believe he is still living, having passed his four score years.

My next visit to the Frenchtown Church, after it was finished, was at a singing school, February 19, 1848. Obadiah Stout, Cyrenius A. Slack and Ambrose Silverthorn were then prominent members.

Camp-meetings were a source of religious enjoyment, and spiritual growth to the society, and large numbers were added during these meetings. The second camp-meeting was held in Francis Roberson's woods, near David Cline's, somewhere near the year 1818, but I have not the names of the preachers who took part.

A camp-meeting was held in the woods. of James Dalrymple, near Joseph Stout's, soon after this. Later still a meeting was held a little north of Croton, also for several seasons, near High Bridge and Califon, and in the woods a little west of the fair ground, near Flemington, where I first attended.

In 1841 a camp-meeting was held on John Slater's, now Pearson Wood's, farm, where I attended meetings, although I cannot recall the names of the preachers. In 1845, a woods meeting, which continued for some days, was held a little east of James Ashcroft's residence. The meeting was removed to the house of Thomas Roberson, where it was continued. Rev. A. K. Street took part in some of these meetings. He now resides in Camden, N. J., and is near ninety years of age.

Sarah Roberson, mother-in-law of Rev. A. K. Street, died March 15th, 1880. This sister was within two months of ninety years old. She was converted in 1817 at a camp-meeting held in Warren County, N. J., under the ministry of Rev. Manning Force. Her house, near Baptisttown was for a long while a home for Methodist preachers, and also a place for holding services. She first joined the Kingwood M. E. Church, but after her husband's death transferred her membership to Frenchtown.

September 12th and 13th, I attended the camp-meeting in the woods, a mile northeast of Frenchtown, on what is now Samuel Opdyke's farm. This was the last camp-meeting held near Frenchtown.

Methodism has become a power for good in our land, and in a little over a century many have been converted to God.

Reminiscences by Rev. A. M. Palmer.

The Rev. Zerubbabel Gaskill was the preacher on Quakertown circuit in 1843-'44. During his second year, I think, a lot was secured in Frenchtown for a church. There was not money on hand to erect and complete the church, and the members and friends did the next best thing. The frame was raised and enclosed, the floor laid and windows and doors put in. Temporary seats were put in the enclosure, somewhat in the order of seating groves in that day for camp-meetings. Quite rustic in appearance, but answered for the time. A platform was built with some of the unplaned boards for a pulpit, and other boards were placed in position for an altar. Two stoves were put in and quite a comfortable place for worship secured. Brother Z. Gaskill preached for several months, every other Sabbath afternoon, in the unfinished room. At the conference in 1845, the Bishop in reading the appointments read, "Quakertown circuit, Abraham M. Palmer." I did not know at the moment in what part of the conference territory I would find my field of labor; but quite soon Brother Gaskill handed me a "plan of the circuit." I found that it was a "two weeks' circuit." One Sabbath I was to preach in the morning at Quakertown and in the afternoon at Cherryville; the following Sabbath at Everittstown in the morning and Frenchtown in the afternoon. This was my first appointment as a married man. I had been married some two months before. As a single man I had preached for three years, remaining but one year on the same charge, as was the custom at that time. My predecessor on the circuit had resided at Quakertown. For the residence of the preacher in 1845 the stewards had rented a house in Frenchtown. May 15th, 1845, at about six o'clock in the afternoon, after a ride of fifty miles, we drove into Frenchtown. My young wife's brother and sister came with us from her father's with his horses and wagon. We brought a few things with us toward housekeeping. I had shipped from Newark a barrel of dishes and two bedsteads, which came to hand the following day. The house was barren of every scrap of furniture which, however, was not uncommon at that time in our parsonages, and especially so in hired houses. I remember till this day my feelings as we stood—the four of us—in that empty house, tired, hungry, lonesome. In a few minutes, however, several persons were at the house to welcome us, and to invite us to supper and lodging. Brother and sister Slack preferred to accommodate the four of us. The next day I bought a cooking stove, a table and a few other things, and we had dinner in our own house and by night had arranged for sleeping. On Sunday, May 18th, I preached at Everittstown in the morning and at Frenchtown in the afternoon; the following Sabbath, at Quakertown in the morning and had a funeral in the afternoon. Soon after coming to Frenchtown I bought a horse, carriage and harness and felt well equipped for my work. Congregations increasingly good and the spiritual interest seemed most excellent during the summer months. On September 3d, we commenced a woods meeting in a grove on the road to Baptisttown. There was much interest in the meetings from the opening. On Sunday, September 7th, the Rev. C. A. Lippencott (in the forenoon) preached a most powerful sermon to a large congregation, and in the afternoon the Lord helped me greatly in preaching to the people. The Holy Spirit was present in mighty saving power. A large number came to the altar for prayer, and ten professed conversion. The meetings were continued in the grove afternoons, and evenings at Brother Thomas Roberson's, and fifty professed conversion. Greater displays of saving power are seldom witnessed. The churches of different denominations for miles were moved to engage in revival work and in some churches there were very many accessions. Sabbath afternoon, October 19th, we had a baptismal service at Frenchtown which was witnessed by a multitude of people. Some fifty kneeled on the bank of the river near the bridge, and I sprinkled water from the river upon their heads in the name of the Father and of the Son and of the Holy Ghost, consecrating them to Christ and his service. Four persons by their special request were immersed in the same adorable name and for the same sacred purpose. In October we had extra meetings at Everittstown and some twenty-five professed conversion. In November, special services were held in Quakertown, and about thirty came into the church on probation. In the fall of 1845, while the revival spirit was abroad, strenuous efforts were made to collect money to finish the Frenchtown church. It was a difficult thing to do. Our members had but little money; we raised what we could, and secured a brother to go abroad and obtain if possible, money to assist us. After a time we felt justified in going forward in the work and rejoiced greatly as the work advanced toward the completion. Wednesday, December 17th, 1845, the church was dedicated. The Presiding Elder, Rev. Isaac Winner preached in the forenoon and dedicated the church. Rev. Abraham Owen, then pastor at New Germantown, preached in the evening. It was a day of rejoicing and one of much interest. In February and March, special services were held in the church and over fifty persons professed conversion. Our conference in the spring of 1846 was held in the Clinton Street Church, Newark; I was ordained Elder at that conference, and was re-appointed to Quakertown circuit; I found much to do in looking after the recent converts and in the general work of the large circuit. In September and October, special meetings were held in Everittstown, and forty persons professed conversion. In November, I held extra meetings in Quakertown; grandly successful, but cut off by storms and bad roads. In January the special meetings in Frenchtown resulted in a goodly number of conversions. In all our revival meetings the members of the church were greatly benefited, and some of them professed entire sanctification. The last page of my diary at Frenchtown, written April

12th, 1847, reads: "Have worked constantly for two years; feel weary in body; hope for a light charge next year; including backsliders reclaimed, over two hundred have been converted at our altar; have not received much money, not enough for our necessities, but friends have been very kind in giving us provisions, some families keeping us bountifully supplied with eatables. We must remember Frenchtown for numerous reasons, and especially as the birthplace of our dear son."

Reminiscenses by Rev. Walter Chamberlin.

Frenchtown first appears in the minutes of 1854 as a station, with James Harris as pastor, but after that year it was connected with Milford till 1861, when I was sent there, when it was again made a station with about one hundred members. I was instructed and almost commanded, by the Presiding Elder, C. S. Vancleve, to see to it that the church be rebuilt and enlarged. I arrived in Frenchtown an entire stranger, Friday evening, April 12th, and put up with the old pastor, George H. Jones.

I preached my first sermon the following Sabbath from Romans, 10: 1. The following Thursday we moved the family, via. Trenton, amidst the excitement of war; the Sixth Massachusetts Regiment passing us as we stood on the platform of the railroad station at Trenton. We were cordially received by the brethren and sisters, who assisted our getting settled in the parsonage. Notwithstanding the war excitement, and some of our young men enlisting to put down the wicked Rebellion, the trustees met on the 10th of May and resolved that a subscription be opened to rebuild and enlarge the church edifice, and as soon as this subscription would warrant, to commence the work in the fear of God. On the 31st of May the trustees and building committees met and resolved to commence the renovation of the church. On June 3d the seats were removed from the church to a hall, and the work began. The church was raised one story, extended in length and a tower put up, with a fine toned bell. (The following letter is inserted by D. M. M.)

"TROY BELL FOUNDRY, January 13th, 1862.

M. E. CHURCH, FRENCHTOWN,
    BY REV. W. CHAMBERLIN,

Bought of JONES & Co.,

1 Church Bell, 710 lbs., @ 30cts....................................	$213 00
Hangings Complete..	35 00
	248 00
Less Donation..	14 20
	$233 80

The above mentioned bell and its mountings are warranted not to break in one year from date and tone warranted satisfactory to the purchaser. Should they fail or break during the year, we agree to recast the bell or replace the broken mountings without charge.

Dated Troy, January 13th, 1862.

JONES & Co.

REV. W. CHAMBERLIN.

DEAR SIR:—Your favor of the 10th was received Saturday, and to-day we ship the bell. Above is bill and warrantee, and inclosed is railroad receipt. This railroad now refuses to contract beyond its own route, and all we could do was to get terms to New York. Please pay that amount and deduct from the bill, viz : 30c. per 100 lbs., on 1,050 lbs , $3.15. We trust the bell will reach you safely and in good time and give you and your people most ample satisfaction. Don't use over a ? rope and the bell will work the better. You will much oblige us by remitting as promptly as convenience will allow.

Very Sincerely Yours,

JONES & Co."

The lecture room was dedicated on Saturday, August 24th, 1861, Rev. C. H. Whiticar preaching in the morning and Rev. William W. Voorhees in the evening. The subscription for the day was $112. On the following day (Sabbath) Rev. Charles E. Hill preached a regular evangelical sermon which was a real benediction to all that heard it. In the afternoon at half-past three o'clock, the Presiding Elder, C. S. Vancleve preached a splendid sermon, and in the evening Rev. W. E. Blakeslee preached for us. The subscription during the two days amounted to about $150.

The dedication of the audience room took place on Tuesday, January 28th, 1862. Bishop E. S. Janes preaching in the morning, Rev. A. K. Street in the afternoon and Dr. I. W. Wiley giving us a grand discourse in the evening. By collection and subscription $500 were raised during the day, leaving $450 to be provided for. The people did nobly considering the circumstances and deserve the prosperity following their sacrifices. Among those worthy of mention was Joseph Ashton, who started the subscription with $100, and finding it a blessing to give, added $50 more. May the blessing of Heaven ever rest on the M. E. Church of Frenchtown !

It may be of interest to you and all the citizens of Frenchtown, to know the age of those trees in front of the church and parsonage. I assisted in planting them Saturday, May 3d, 1862.

Reminiscences by Rev. C. Clark, Jr.

When I came to my pastorate, the people of Frenchtown had just voted no license for the borough; and in consequence of which we were a dry town for that year. It was during the panic of '71 that the license people thought they saw the business of the town prostrate, and "grass growing in the streets," and in the spring election, secured a majority in the council for license again. Of course, grass did not grow in the streets, neither had it before, but drunkenness, disorder and noise did result therefrom.

During my third year, the town and church were visited by a most remarkable and overwhelming revival of religion; and a few facts leading thereto may be worthy of mention. My health was in such a precarious condition that my advisers urged upon me positive rest; but my conviction was that there must be a meeting held, and I arranged for it about as follows: I called for volunteers among the ladies to go under my direction two by two and canvass the town, and do strictly pastoral work of religious conversation and prayer. Six ladies, including my wife, responded to the call. They met at the old parsonage, and an hour was devoted to consecration and prayer. It was a holy hour! Each one felt that God was in the plan, and that it must succeed; and with this feeling and a baptism of the Holy Spirit, this faithful little band began their labors from house to house.

I had arranged with the officials of the church, that they should conduct the singing and praying and to work in the congregation, and leave me to take it as easy as circumstances would permit, and to secure ministerial aid if deemed necessary; but in less than a week it became apparent that no assistant preachers would be necessary to further the glorious work.

The basement of the church was thronged with anxious humanity, and the altar with weeping penitents. The work of that consecrated band of women during the first afternoon was clearly visible at the evening service.

Soon the subject for conversation in the stores, shops and hotels of the town was the revival in the Methodist Church; and as a consequence, all classes and persuasions flocked to the meetings and some remarkable scenes took place. Many members of the church soon found that they needed more grace for the work, and held a holiness meeting for that purpose. Members of the Presbyterian and Baptist churches stood up for prayer and came to the altar and sought a state of justification which they declared they had never before enjoyed. Thus for one month or more these services engrossed the thought and conversation of the town and vicinity, and resulted in the addition of some seventy-five persons of all ages to the membership of the church.

At the conclusion of this series of meetings, the question of license or no license came up again. I consulted with the Rev. C. Conkling, a retired Presbyterian minister residing in the town concerning the matter, and the result was a call for a meeting of especially selected citizens in the basement of our church to consider the question. This was indeed a memorable meeting, both for its personal character and for the decided spirit manifested for God and the right. The result was that a committee of thirteen was appointed with authority to make a ticket for the approaching election for mayor and councilmen, and to report in one week for approval. The selection made by the committee was highly satisfactory, and we pledged ourselves to work for the ticket. The liquor men had been demoralized by the revival, but boasted of being victorious; but when the votes were counted they were badly defeated, and the church and no license reigned again for one year at least.

My pastorate at Frenchtown was very pleasant, both in its social and church relationship. I could mention the names of many with whom I was associated, and with whom I passed many hours of spiritual and social profit; but for fear of occupying too much space, I shall refrain from so doing. Some of those associates have gone to heaven; some have moved to other earthly homes; but there are many who yet reside in the town. Those names are dear to me; and I shall ever hold in fond remembrance the personalities they represent, and the happy scenes entwined around them—scenes undimmed by the haze and mist of the years that have since flown.

But if permitted, I shall make mention of one man; Morris Maxwell, class leader; I believe it was so before I came and after I left; I know it to be true during my stay, that Brother Maxwell was most faithful to his duty as class leader. He led a class meeting in the church, and he led it rain or shine. On the night of his meeting it was a well-known fact throughout the town that he could always be found at the Methodist Church with his class. Sometimes few and sometimes many met with this good man, and all found it "good to be there."

The closing hours of my stay in the town were exceedingly pleasant. Many persons came to assist us in packing and getting off, and we left the parsonage for the station, believing we had said good-bye to nearly all. To our surprise, however, the station was thronged in and out with members of the church and others. It was a hallowed moment of hand-shaking, tears and good wishes never to be forgotten.

Reminiscences by Rev. Joseph Gaskill.

The following was published in *The Hunterdon Independent*, June 22d, 1894. It was written as a supplement to a paper read at Frenchtown before the Hunterdon County Historical Society :

Editor of *The Hunterdon Independent*.

DEAR SIR :— Will you please allow me a little space in your valuable paper to supplement, or add to, that very remarkable history, of the rise and progress of the Methodist Episcopal Church in Frenchtown, as written by the Rev. D. M. Matthews, and published in your paper, *The Independent*, of June the 8th inst. ; and also, to give some brief account of my ministry in the adjoining community to Frenchtown in the year of 1842 ? But first of all, I want to thank you, or to whoever it was that sent me the paper that contained the graphic history ; and also, Brother Matthews who wrote it in such detail, fullness and general accuracy. I have read the communication with great pleasure, and have no criticisms or corrections to make, save *one* ; and that is only in the date, or year, when the " first class " or society was formed in Frenchtown.

Mr. Matthews says, " In 1840 the first class was formed in Frenchtown by Joseph Gaskill." That is a mistake, whereas it was formed in 1842. I was admitted into the New Jersey Annual Conference in the month of April, 1842, and was appointed, as the minutes of the Conference show, to Quakertown charge ; the charge consisted of four appointments, namely, Quakertown, Everittstown, Baptisttown and Kingwood.

This charge had formerly been a part of old Flemington circuit, but at the conference had been set off by itself, and I was appointed as its *first pastor*. I entered upon the work with some misgivings as a young man of little experience, and moderate intellectual abilities, but, being filled with " faith and the Holy Ghost " I had but little doubt as to the outcome.

In addition to the four churches demanding my time and labor, I began to study, and plan how to reach the masses of the non-church-going people. Accordingly in the month of August I arranged to hold a woods meeting near Quakertown for a few days. In the meantime I had secured the promise of old Brother Banghart, (of precious memory) Presiding Elder on Newton district, to help me in the meeting, and preach for me, especially Sunday. When Sunday morning came, a large concourse of people were gathered, and Father Banghart was on hand, and took for his text the words of the weeping prophet Jeremiah. " Rivers of water runneth down mine eyes, etc."; and from the announcement of the text he began to weep, and throughout the sermon his cheeks were bathed in tears; and among the masses of the great congregation there was scarcely a dry eye. Under that sermon, many were awakened, many hearts were melted, and not a few were happily saved from their sins.

Have all the weeping prophets and preachers passed away? Has the *cause* ceased to exist? or have preachers and people become so refined, educated and hardened that the fountain of tears is dried up?

Not being able to continue the meeting in the grove longer, I concluded to follow up the good work by opening and inviting the people to the church at Quakertown, to which they came in crowds and packed the house night after night, and the revival continued with unabated interest until I was stricken down with disease, and had to close the meeting; but as it was quite a large number were saved and the church was greatly comforted.

After recovering from my illness, and still filled with an irrepressible desire for new conquests, and not feeling content to confine my labors to my immediate charge alone, I resolved to venture out into the "regions beyond" if need be, and learning that Frenchtown, a few miles from Baptisttown, had no church, or church organization of any kind, and also hearing that there was *one man at least* who was in favor of having religious service held in the place; and as the doors of the school-house were closed against all ministerial intruders, he proposed to open his shop for the purpose. So, learning this fact, I made it a point to have an appointment given out for me to preach there on a given Sabbath afternoon, and when the hour arrived I think there were present about a score of souls, men, women and children.

During the service, I thought there were indications that they would like me to preach again, so I gave out another appointment for two weeks from that day. When the two weeks rolled round, a still larger gathering was present, and I tried as best I could to give them some plain gospel truths, and impress upon them the importance of at once consecrating their hearts and lives to God and his service then and there forever. And being encouraged by visible effects, I gave out a third appointment for two weeks, and on this occasion I made the strongest appeal to them I was capable of to make a start for the kingdom, and identify themselves at once with the people and church of God; and at the close of the service, I called for volunteers to join the church on probation, and eleven men and women came forward and gave me their names, and I recorded them in a class book prepared for that purpose; and appointed old Brother Thomas Robertson, of Baptisttown, as their leader, and Ambrose Silverthorn assistant. *That* was the origin, and beginning of the organization of the Methodist Episcopal Church in the Borough of Frenchtown.

Truly it was the day of small things; humble the beginning, but what has God wrought during these more than fifty years?

The seed planted had vitality in itself, took deep root, and sprang up and has born abundant fruitage. To God be all the glory.

At the close of this conference year '42, I was removed from Quakertown charge and sent to Gloucester circuit, embracing twenty-one appointments, 1,100 members, with Joseph Atwood as my colleague; and of course, the little infant church at Frenchtown fell into the hands of my successor, and subsequently his successors to the present time. How well they have nourished and cared for the tender infant plant, Brother Matthews' glowing history fully sets forth. To God be all the glory for this wonderful result.

I would like to make mention of a revival also that took place at Everittstown during the winter of '42; quite a number were converted; among them, some few arose to distinction and usefulness. There was Sylvester Opdyke, who became a member of the Newark Conference, and Presiding Elder; but he has passed to his reward. There was also one by the name of Mahlon Rittenhouse; I think he is still living, and a merchant at Everittstown; and still others whose names have faded from my memory; but their names were written in Heaven, and I trust they remain uneffaced.

A short time before I left my charge for conference, I held a little extra meeting in a neighborhood called the swamp, about three or four miles south of Quakertown, where some twelve or fifteen souls were brought to the Saviour. With this extra service, in connection with the regular work of the charge I closed up the year. It was a year of much sacrifice, of hard toil, but full of blessing to my soul.

For this year's labor I received all told, one hundred and twenty dollars, and riches of grace added thereto.

It may seem to you in reading the above narrative, and to your readers, that I betray much egotism, but this is far from me; I could not give you the facts without making myself prominent   J. G.

TRENTON, N. J., June 13th, 1894.

4

CHAPTER V.

BRIEF PERSONAL SKETCHES OF THE PASTORS WHO HAVE SERVED THE FRENCHTOWN M. E. CHURCH.

Behold, a sower went forth to sow: And when he sowed, some seeds fell by the wayside, and the fowls came and devoured them up: But others fell into good ground, and brought forth fruit, some a hundred fold, some sixty fold, some thirty fold.—Bible.

Joseph Gaskill.

PERSONAL sketch of the life and ministry of Rev. Joseph Gaskill. The name of my father was Jacob Gaskill and the name of my mother Sarah Gaskill, her maiden name being Sarah Bass. I was born at Hanover Furnace, in Burlington County, N. J., in the year of our Lord, December 3d, 1817. One year after I was born my father bought a tavern property and connected therewith a farm, five miles west of the Furnace, and moved with the family to this place, then called Centerville, (but now Pointville). Here I lived till I became twenty-one years of age.

Centerville was so called for the reason six public roads converged to a central point. The tavern, then so called, was more a place for travelers and entertainment than a saloon. This village was located near the line that divided the open oak farming country, and the pine region. The youth of this community were not favored with the best educational and religious advantages, however, we had a common district school and occasionally religious services. The house located here, was used for both purposes. This place then was included as an appointment on New Egypt circuit, and the preachers came once in two weeks and proclaimed the Gospel to a small membership of Methodist people comprising one class. On Sunday a local preacher sometimes preached the word, at other times a prayer meeting was held, and always the class was kept up uniformly and regularly.

Occasionally I attended some of these services, but never made a start for the kingdom, although I was subject nearly all the time to the keenest compunction for sin.

This condition of affairs remained till the year 1837, when the Rev.

REV. JOSEPH GASKILL.
(See Page 11.)

Thomas G. Stewart, of blessed memory, came on the New Egypt circuit, and as a herald of fire he went around the circuit, and everywhere revivals took place, and hundreds were converted; and last of all he came to our little chapel and opened his batteries, and preached with such unction, and power, and plead with tears with the ungodly to flee from the wrath to come, and many broke down and rushed to the altar, and three of my sisters were among them. My feelings were stirred, my heart seemed to melt like wax before the fire, and my head became a fountain of tears; but I strove against the spirit and finally suppressed my emotions, and dried my tears, and came off victor for the time. The next day (Thursday) as I was at work near the tavern, I looked up and saw Father Steward approaching, and soon he dismounted from his horse, and to my surprise at once went into the sitting-room where my mother and sisters were. For a moment I thought it an unusual thing for a minister to visit a tavern; I thought I would like to know what the preacher had to say to mother and sisters, yet I did not want him to see me, but the thought struck me, I can hear him without his seeing me; so I went to the house and entered the cellar by the outside door and went up the cellar steps that led to the sitting-room, and planting myself by the door and putting my ear to the crack, I could hear distinctly the minister talking to my mother and sisters. After a little he proposed to pray, and they all bowed down. O, how earnestly he prayed and pleaded with God for the family and for the children especially by name, for some one had given him all our first names. When he held me up before God by name, I wilted and fairly broke down, then the spirit said, " Now or never, now or never;" I said, " Lord I yield, I yield, I can hold out no more." So from the cellar I immediately went to the barn and there with God I cried and prayed for mercy and salvation, but with little comfort, except I was sure pardon was in reserve for me. From that Thursday morning I continued to pray, but without light or peace until the following Sunday afternoon. In the morning I went to the prayer meeting, but found no relief; I returned home, took a Bible, went up to the garret of the old tavern, threw myself on a bed and commenced to read the fifth chapter of Matthew; when I came to the verse, " Blessed are they that mourn," etc., I paused a moment and said, that is I, I mourn, the comfort is for me; suddenly effulgent light filled the old garret, and joyful peace filled my believing soul. All glory to God for my salvation through the instrumentality of Rev. Thomas G. Steward.

A few days after I was converted, walking out in the evening for meditation and prayer, something seemed to say to me you must

preach the Gospel, and at the thought I was overwhelmed with joy,
but soon after another thought rushed into my mind and said, you are
greatly mistaken about this preaching business, it is all a delusion, the
work is of your imagination.   The idea of your being a preacher without an education. It is folly. The suggestion seemed very plausible and a
matter of fact ; so I let the subject rest and gave it no further thought,
but continued to pray and live a Christian as aforetime, but somehow I
began to lose ground ; I did not find access to the throne, or realize the
joy of the Lord, or the witness of the spirit, and fell into doubt and
fear, so I was led to cry to God for help and mercy. While praying,
the same messenger came to me again and said with increased
emphasis, you must preach; and in my agony I said, anything, Lord, so
I can have restored to my soul thy salvation : then I was again made
unspeakably happy. From this time I began to make some preparation for the great work. Up to this time I had only attended our
common district school, but in the ensuing fall and winter I went to
the Wrightstown school, and the next spring the trustees of our school
wished me to take and teach their school.   I thought it would give me
some advantages for study, so I took the school, got along with it nicely,
and I think gave general satisfaction.   During the year Brother Petherbridge, the Presiding Elder, came to me one day and said: "Jose,
I want you to preach on the circuit Sundays regularly with the other
preachers, and they will fill the week-day appointments and you can
drive on your school through the week. Brother Webb will furnish
you a horse and bridle;" I said, "Brother, I do not know about
preaching."   "Well," he said "go and try."

I feared to refuse, and when the next Sunday morning came I went
over to Brother Webb's and found the horse ready; I mounted, and
away I started for my first appointment with fear and trembling as to
the outcome; I continued in the work and school for the balance of the year, nearly nine months. The record I made on
the circuit may be judged by the fact that at the last quarterly conference of the year the conference recommended me
to be received into the annual conference of New Jersey, without my asking or knowledge until after it was done. I could but
appreciate the favor and their confidence in me and returned my hearty
thanks ; but it was a question with me as to whether I enter the
ministry at once or tarry for a time, and go to school for better
preparation. After due consideration I concluded to go to Pennington
Seminary at least for a season. I remained at the Seminary part of
the years' 1841-'42, and at the last quarterly conference of Pennington
charge of '42, I was recommended again to the annual conference of

New Jersey, and was received and sent to Quakertown charge as already stated in a former paper. (See reminiscences.)

Some two years prior to the meeting of the annual conference I had engaged to marry a young lady by the name of Mary Cliver, a daughter of a farmer living near Wrightstown, Burlington Co., N. J. This was a question of much thought to me, as to the time when this episode should come off. So, as I knew Father Petherbridge was my warm friend, I consulted him in reference to the matter, and he readily advised me to marry as soon as we wished; being encouraged to take this step, we were married some two weeks before the sitting of the conference, by our pastor, Rev. James Long. When the conference assembled, I with other young ministers appeared, and as the proper time had come to consider their cases for admission, my name was called and the usual question asked, "is he married or single." Father Petherbridge, my former Presiding Elder, responded, "He is married, and I would rather have him married than single," so the motion was made for my admission and carried without a dissenting voice. At the close of the session my name was read for Quakertown. Among the many things that occurred during the year under my ministry that has afforded me great pleasure, was that memorable day when I preached my third and last sermon in Frenchtown, and at the close I invited persons to join the church when eleven men and women gave me their names and I enrolled them in a book for that purpose. That was the origin and start of the Methodist Episcopal Church in Frenchtown. I was allowed to remain on this charge but one year, and from there I was sent to Gloucester circuit, Gloucester County, of twenty-one appointments and fourteen hundred members with Joseph Atwood as my colleague. From this circuit I was sent to Cedarville, and from Cedarville to Cumberland circuit, from there to Cape May circuit, from there to Swedesboro circuit, and then to Pittsgrove, Salem County; then Fairfield, Essex County; then to Madison, (the seat of the Theological Seminary), then to Sharpetown, Salem County, and from here suffice it to say, I went into other fields of labor and continued in the work as health and circumstances permitted. During these years of toil some hundreds of souls were gathered into the fold and some already have been housed in the heavenly garner, all of which I hope will be stars in my crown of rejoicing in the world of spirits. My precious wife entered the itinerancy with me in high hope and endured the hardships and privations with Christian fortitude and patience incident to such a life, and helped to bear my burdens, and cheerfully and tenderly nursed me through much sickness that fell to my lot. She was spared to me forty-six years to care for me, and seven years ago she was suddenly stricken down and peacefully passed away. Six children were born to us, three of whom died in infancy; the others grew to maturity, but while young they were all happily converted to God and joined the church. My oldest son entered the army during the Rebellion and soon fell a victim by disease, and I trust he died a victor; my other and youngest son was seized with disease and died at the age of twenty. My only child and daughter still lives to be the light and joy of my home. I am now in my seventy-eighth year and I am looking forward to the time of deliverance and cherish a sure and certain hope of entering through the pearly gate to sit down with the good and happy throng, where the wicked cease to trouble and the weary are at rest.

Zerubbabel Gaskill.

On the 13th of November, 1852, our Brother, Zerubbabel Gaskill, departed this life in the city of Philadelphia, at the house of his brother, aged forty-eight. He was blessed with that special blessing, *a pious mother*. In his eleventh year he was converted to God, in his seventeenth year he joined the M. E. Church, at Newport, N. J., then under the ministry of the Rev. John Creamer, of precious memory. In 1833 he was called to fill a vacancy in the Salem circuit, N. J. In 1834 he joined the Philadelphia Conference, and was appointed to Moorestown circuit, N. J.; 1835, Smyrna, Del.; 1836, Caroline, Md.; 1837-'38, Bargaintown, N. J.; 1839, Crosswicks; 1840, Crosswicks and Bethel Mission; 1841-'42, Middletown Point; 1843-'44, Quakertown circuit; 1845-'46, Haddonfield; 1847-'48, Blackwoodtown circuit; 1849-'50, Tuckerton circuit; 1851-'52, Clarksboro, where his labors and suffering ceased. The text selected for his funeral discourse, Act xi: 24; "For he was a good man, full of the Holy Ghost and of faith," is a very fit illustration of Brother Gaskill's character as a minister. Though he might not have been considered brilliant, yet he possessed all the substantial qualifications this sacred text imports. The substratum of his thoughts was strong and pertinent, and had he possessed the grace of delivery, he would have been considered among our strong men in the pulpit. His life exemplified the text. *Consistency* and *fervor* were marked characteristics in him. We do not know that he possessed what some have called the *divine art*, yet he loved sacred verse. On Sabbath, when near his end, and contemplating the holy temples of the Lord, and the gathering together of the people, he repeated these expressive lines:

> "Thousands, O Lord of Hosts, this day
>   Around Thine altars meet,
> And tens of thousands throng to pay
>   Their homage at Thy feet."

> "Deprived I am,"

but continued—

> "I may not to Thy courts repair,
>   Yet here Thou *surely art*,
> Lord consecrate a home of prayer
>   In my surrendered heart."

Contemplating death, he exclaimed:

> "How shall I meet this foe
>   Whose frown my soul alarms?
> Dark horror sits upon his brow,
>   And victory waits his arms!

He answered—

> "But with an eye of faith,
>   Peering beyond the grave,
> I see that friend who conquered death,
>   Whose arm alone can save."

In conversation with a brother in the ministry a little before his departure, he said he was very happy, and praised the Lord; and when raised up a little, he said: "Let me go. Hallelujah! Praise the Lord!" and calmly folding his hands upon his bosom, he ceased to breath. Brother Gaskill has left a wife and four children to mourn their irreparable loss; and the church has lost a faithful minister.

To Thy behest, great God, we bow.—*New Jersey Conference Minutes.*

Abraham M. Palmer.

Abraham M. Palmer was born in White Plains, New York, November 30th, 1817. His parents were Richard C., and Susan B. Palmer. Both were well known, and prominent in the community and in the church. His mother was a quiet, godly woman, dearly beloved. His father was the first class-leader in the church at White Plains, and for sixty-five years a licensed exhorter and was "abundant in labors." He held several of the most important positions in his township and county. Both were spared for many years, his father being ninety-five at his death. His father was a merchant in early life, and Abraham M. expected to follow his father in the mercantile business and received a good business education.

His religious life had an early beginning; he believes that he was truly converted at twelve years of age, but at that time boys of his age were thought to be too young to unite with the church. Thanks be to God it is not so now.

In March 1835, he received a clerkship in New York City, and very soon thereafter united with the Allen Street Methodist Episcopal Church and Sunday-school. His church, Sabbath-school and class-meetings were dearly prized and he was seldom absent. A few years after uniting with the church he was deeply impressed with the thought that the ministry was to be his life-work. The thought was not in harmony with his desires. Flattering financial prospects were before him, and he had reached the first position in a large dry goods house, and had the promise of an early promotion to a partnership in the business.

In 1840, the impression ripened into a positive conviction and call from God to the work of the ministry which he dared not resist. "Woe is unto me if I preach not the Gospel." God said it to him, and he began to make special plans for his life-work. He entered upon a preparatory course of study intending to enter college in the fall of 1842.

At that time young men were in special demand for the ministry, many of the large circuits had been cut up into small stations and single men only could be supported. In the spring of 1842, he was persuaded by prominent ministers in the church, to abandon his proposed college course, and enter the ministry at once and pursue his studies as best he could. Mr. Wesley's words were frequently repeated to him, "Gaining knowledge is a good thing, but saving souls is a better."

In April 1842, he was received into the New Jersey Conference and stationed at Fort Lee. His appointments after the above date were as follows: Parsippany, Bethel, Quakertown, Everittstown and French-town, Lambertville, Belvidere, First Church Phillipsburg, Newark, three of the leading churches on Staten Island, Jersey City, Plainfield and others.

In 1892, he closed his fifty years in the effective work without a break; he then asked for a supernumary relation, and removed to Newark where he now resides.

He has been blessed during his ministry with many gracious revivals and probably has received over two thousand persons into the church.

He has superintended the building of six new churches and three parsonages, and the repairing and beautifying of many others.

He has been especially successful in paying church debts, which in

REV. ABRAHAM M. PALMER.
(See Page 51.)

some cases were very embarrassing to the success of the respective churches.

Three times he has been sent by the Bishops to settle painful difficulties in prominent churches, and has been called the " peacemaker " of his conference.

He has been treasurer of his conference for thirty-two years, and probably over a million of dollars passed through his hands to the several benevolent societies without the loss of a dollar, or any cost to the church.

Thomas T. Campfield.

Rev. Thomas Thornton Campfield was born in Hagerstown, Maryland, May 23d, 1811. His father died when he was only three years old. In his eighth year we find him a resident of Freehold, Monmouth County, N. J., in the neighborhood of which he continued to reside until he entered upon his itinerating career. After traveling several years under the Presiding Elder, he was admitted on trial in the New Jersey Conference, at Trenton, April 20th, 1844. He died suddenly at Washington, Warren County, N. J., April 14th, 1885. At the same conference, seventeen others entered with him ; eight of whom have fallen in the ranks.

He filled the following appointments in the New Jersey and the Newark conferences : Mount Zion, 1844-'45 ; Lambertville, 1846 ; Quakertown, 1847-'48 ; Flanders, 1849-'50 ; Springfield and Westfield, 1851-'52 ; Westfield, 1853-'54 ; Frenchtown and Milford, 1855-'56 ; Peapack and Cross-roads, 1857-'58 ; Somerville, 1859-'60 ; Springfield again, 1861-'62 ; Anderson and Mount Bethel, 1863 ; Mount Bethel and Oxford Furnace, 1864 ; Harmony, 1865-'66 ; Broadway, 1867-'69 ; Union and Pattenburg, 1870-'72 ; Springville and New Village, 1873-'75 ; Pleasant Valley, 1876-'78 ; Mount Bethel and Beattystown, 1879-'80.

At the conference in the spring of 1881, his effective work of thirty-seven years in the conference closed, and he retired to the supernumerary line. Some twelve years before he entered the ministry he had married Miss Ruhannah Smith, of Freehold, August 30th, 1832, with whom he lived nineteen years. On May 21st, 1856, he married Miss Fannie A. Kemple, of Hackettstown, who shared his toil for twenty-four years. He married, March 15th, 1882, Miss Maggie M. Cummins, also of Hackettstown.

These are a few outlines of the life of our departed brother. Each line is deserving of a fuller notice. We can only satisfy ourselves of some of the more salient features of his character. And first of all, he had a

clear, strong and convincing proof of sins forgiven, which he held
to through all his varied life as the strict anchor of his soul. He had
studied the Book of God as the sole fountain of faith, and faith as the
essential condition of the justification of his nature. His call to the
ministry followed soon after this mighty change. He knew his acquired
abilities were limited for the great work before him. He knew he
could not enter into any regular schools of the prophets, for there were
none. The church he loved and had been instrumental in his conversion, had not yet opened the gates of these grand institutions to candi-
dates seeking literary culture and theological training. In fact, the
voice of the church was then against such drill. The "Bush College"
was the order of the day. What was he to do? Check his convictions
of imperative duty? Remain at home? Continue in the use of the
hoe, the axe, the spade, or to follow the plow and till the soil? "No,"
he said; "I must go and preach the Gospel." He knew that a knowledge of disease alone does not make a man a physician; it shows him
how to apply the remedies which another science has made known to
him. He says, "I can by divine grace describe the sin malady, and
point the struggling soul to the all-healing fountain." He had tasted
the fruit of life and knew how to recommend it to others. He had
found the kernel in the nut, the wheat in the husk, the marrow in the
bones. Will the church now call him into her vineyard? This question
was not immediately answered. He was a married man, and thirty-
four years old. Married men were not then so readily admitted into
the conference. We remember the discussion—the suspense—the patient
waiting before the favorable response was given. He entered, and for
more than forty odd years he cut his way through the forest, plowed
deep furrows and left in them the seeds of a great harvest.

He had in him evidently a heroic spirit. We claim, if the harder
field of labor or the more dangerous line of battle is the place of honor,
then surely our departed brother was entitled to that distinction. He
was never known to wince or shrink at the word of command. He was
naturally diffident and retiring, but as a captain in Christ's army he
was as bold as a lion. We have often seen him leap into the thickest
of the fight, and have never known him to flinch. His record will
show that he possessed and maintained the truest Christian and ministerial bravery; some of the instances of time and place to illustrate
his heroism have been in past written out by himself and are now
filed away in the archives of our Historical Society. At our last conference, with roll in hand, he said to the writer, "Here is an account
of my life work," and we verily believe when the future historian shall
write of the acts and actors of the Church of God, he will find that in

REV. T. T. CAMPFIELD.

many localities of New Jersey no inconsiderable part was played by T. T. Campfield. The most of us are ready to admit that true ministerial heroism consists very largely in self-sacrifice and self-restraint. Are there any fields neglected, overgrown, abandoned? Who will go? Our brother said, "I will go; send me." He went, esteeming it a great privilege to work anywhere for the Master. He lived on short allowances. His powers of endurance were sometimes taxed to their utmost capacity. He knew how to be abased and how to suffer need, and we have not the least doubt that there are some in our day who would retire if they had to till such fields and do the kind of work this man did in the earlier and later days of his ministry. There are but few men in New Jersey who have builded more churches and erected more parsonages than our departed brother. Thousands were converted through his instrumentality, many of whom are now preaching the Gospel. He labored, and others are now entering into his labors. He sowed and planted, and others are gathering and enjoying the harvest.

Brother Campfield had a peculiar aptness for dates and figures. From these we learned that he traveled in his own conveyance as a minister from March 2d, 1839, to March 2d, 1884—45 years—about 120,000 miles; served twenty-two charges; preached about 7,000 times; made about 12,000 pastoral calls; received into the Methodist Episcopal Church, on probation and into full membership, about 2,057 persons; baptized about 1,000; attended about 700 funerals, and married about 600 couples.

The writer spent a night at his house only a few days before his sudden transition. He spoke of his severe sickness through the winter —how near he came to passing over the river, and how God brought him back as from the gates of death. He referred to the struggle he had in reaching the Conference before the roll-call, saying he had only missed once in forty-one years. We call up the devotional hour of that night before retiring. How happy he seemed; what quick and earnest responses he made as we thanked the Lord for His saving grace, and the triumphs of the Cross through our humble efforts. Evidently God was preparing him for the chariot and the crown. He had done his work. His reward awaited him on high. His classmates loved him; we all loved him. The earth is better for his having lived in it, and heaven is richer for his entrance there. May we be ready when the Bridegroom cometh. May our sunsetting be radiant with peace, and our spirit pass away into the brightness of immortality.

His funeral services were held in the Hackettstown Methodist Episcopal Church, April 18th, 1885, under the charge of J. A. Munroe, his pastor.—*Newark Conference Minutes.*

Rev. S. W. Decker.

Brother Decker was born in Orange County, New York, October 18th, 1807. His parents were exemplary and respectable members of the Old School Presbyterian Church, and brought him up in the fear of the Lord. At an early age he engaged in teaching school. In 1832, he attended a camp-meeting near Flemington, N. J., and heard a sermon by Rev. Charles Pitman, P. E. He and his young wife were thoroughly aroused to a sense of their danger, and sought and found the pearl of great price, and soon after offered themselves as probationers to the M. E. Church, and were received by Rev. J. L. Gilder, late of the N. Y. East Conference.

In 1837, he was licensed to preach. In 1838 Rev. Manning Force, P. E., appointed him as a supply for Springfield. At the Conference in 1839, he was admitted on trial, and returned to Springfield. His subsequent appointments were as follows: 1840, Orange; 1841-'42, New Prospect, where he was engaged in a glorious revival, and hundreds were brought to Christ; 1843-'44, Vernon, Ct.: 1845-'46, Stanhope; 1847-'48, Stillwater; 1849-'50, Quakertown; 1851, New Egypt; while at this last appointment, he was made chaplain to the state prison in Trenton, where he was continued two or three years. To sustain his growing family, he engaged in the mercantile business, and became deeply involved in debt. Greatly embarrassed, and under great mental depression, he withdrew from the ministry, saying, "How can I preach the Gospel when I owe $4,000?" He gave up all his property to his creditors and moved to Jersey City, and, after earnest prayer, he again commenced business, promising, if success attended him, he would pay all his old debts. He was greatly prospered, and, though not legally bound, yet he felt himself morally bound to pay every debt, principal and interest, which he was able to do. This was a noble example of honesty. While in Jersey City such was his godly life, and his religious influence, that the preachers felt he ought to be restored to the Conference, and his name was re-entered upon our Conference roll as a supernumerary with work. He moved from Jersey City to Paterson, and spent the most of his later years in that city, where he was looked upon as a man of God, pure in life, and an efficient worker in the church. He supplied a number of appointments in the vicinity, and was ever ready to work for Christ and souls. He died at Paterson, April 25th, 1884.—*Newark Con. Minutes.*

Rev. S. W. Decker.
(See Page 69.)

Rodney Winans.

The Rev. Rodney Winans was born on Governor's Island, on the 6th day of January, 1813. He died at his home in Branch Mills, near Westfield, New Jersey, September 15th, 1882.

He was converted, and joined the Methodist Episcopal Church, in Newark, in March, 1832. While yet a youth, he became a highly esteemed and useful class-leader. Brother John Scarlett (at that time a professed infidel) was induced to attend his class, and about a year after was converted.

Brother Winans was licensed as a local preacher in 1838, in Carlisle, Pa. He had already entered Dickinson College in 1835. There, by his diligence, he showed his belief that "gaining knowledge is a good thing ;" but he also believed that " the winning of souls is a better." The journal of his student days is largely occupied with accounts of class-meetings, quarterly meetings, and sermons. A good part of his education at Carlisle was the inspiring influence of Dr. Durbin, the President of the college.

He longed to be engaged in the regular work of the ministry, and was received into the New Jersey Conference at its session, held in Bridgeton, April, 1838.

During his active ministry he filled the following appointments : Mendham, Asbury, Cokesbury, Dover and Millbrook, Woodbury, Moorestown, Medford, Haverstraw, Trenton, Quakertown, Clinton, New Providence, Woodbridge, New Dover, Newton, North Haverstraw and Ramapo.

Among his early colleagues were Thomas J. Stewart, George Banghart, Joseph J. Sleeper, and (as his juniors) M. C. Stokes and Charles Lareu.

Dr. Lareu remembers him as remarkable for "the charms of his thought, the keen analysis of his subject, and the conciseness of his expression." His sermons were always thoroughly studied and evangelical. He loved an argument. His mind was naturally metaphysical. Solid theological books (always of the Wesleyan type) were his favorite studies. The thoughtful listeners were always best pleased with his preaching, the tendency of which was rather to the edification of believers than to the awakening of the irreligious. But he continually longed for revivals, and was not infrequently blessed with them. The most notable of these occurred on the Moorestown and Medford circuits, where the people still testify that "his name is as ointment poured forth.--*Newark Con. Minutes.*

Joseph Horner

Was admitted on trial in the New Jersey Conference in 1850, and was sent to Freehold as junior preacher, with J. W. Barrett; Quakertown circuit, including Frenchtown and Everittstown in 1851, with Rodney Winans.

There was a gracious revival of religion at the last named place. J. F. Case, of Everittstown; Joseph Everitt, of Quakertown, and the writer (then of Everittstown), were among the number of converts.

His next appointment was New Prospect. His field of labor in 1854-'55 was Rockland Lake; 1856, Milltown, and in 1857 the minutes return him as supernumerary.

Curtis Talley.

Brother Curtis Talley was born November 19th, 1807, near Wilmington, Delaware, and died at Pennington, New Jersey, December 5th, 1855, aged forty-eight years. His parents were respectable people and his mother was a member of the Methodist Episcopal Church, connected with one of the societies of old Chester circuit, Philadelphia conference. Brother Talley spent his youth at home, dividing his time between labor and books, except a winter or two passed at an academy in a neighboring town. His father's home being not far from one of the regular preaching places on the circuit, he was from his earliest years an attendant on the worship and familiar with the doctrine and ways of the Methodists. In the twenty-third year of his age he was converted and united with the church, and the next year was appointed class-leader and licensed as an exhorter. He was zealous, laborious and acceptable in conducting religious service at the little neighborhood meetings and saw much good done. Two years later, in 1833, at a quarterly meeting held by Lawrence McCombe at the Grove church, he was licensed as a local preacher, and three months afterward at an annual conference was received as a candidate for the itinerant ministry. Brother Talley often referred to his labors as an exhorter and local preacher on Chester circuit. Among his neighbors and friends many souls were converted during the last years of these his early ministrations, and he seemed to regard this period as the happiest, and he sometimes said, the most useful part of his life. One incident, which he used to relate is worthy of record, as an example of the diversities of operation wrought by the same God which worketh all in all. Brother Talley had been conducting a series of meetings at a school-house and a revival was in progress. One evening the room was filled

REV. WM. M. BURROUGHS.

See Page 68

with people and the meeting waxed warmer and warmer. Seven persons were kneeling at a bench seeking the pardon of their sins, while all were engaged in fervent importunate prayer, there came an awakening influence as sudden as the rushing mighty wind and the tongues of fire on the day of Pentecost. Every believer at the same moment felt its power, and either bowed beneath it in speechless rapture, or shouted aloud in an ecstasy of holy joy. At the self-same instant the seven persons seeking peace with God passed from death unto life, and began to weep happy tears, or praise the Lord aloud for his pardoning grace. Brother Talley was received on trial by the Philadelphia Conference in April, 1834. The subsequent appointments were as follows:—1834-'35, Asbury circuit; 1836, Caldwell circuit; 1837, Belleville; 1838, Madison; 1839-'40, Somerville; 1841-'42, Woodbridge; 1843, Perth Amboy; 1844-'45, Crosswicks; 1846,-'47, Nyack; 1848-'49, Springfield; 1850-'51, Pennington; 1852, Rahway; 1853, Quakertown.

In November, 1836, he was united in marriage to Miss Agnes C. Crain. They had one daughter, Helen, the sunshine of the home. Twenty years, as shown above, filled the measure of Brother Talley's life in the effective ministry. For some years previous to his death there were symptoms of pulmonary disease and his health was gradually declining. He struggled on however, hoping against hope, until at last his disease became so aggravated that he could no longer hide from his own eyes the fact that he must seek at least a temporary respite from labor, and at the New Brunswick session of the New Jersey Conference in 1854, he was constrained to ask a supernumerary relation. The love of life was strong within him, and love for the work of the ministry was even stronger.

As the weary months passed on and strength declined, and while the cough of the consumptive grew more and more hollow and painful, he clung to the idea that he should yet return to the work with new energies of body and soul. In the last stage of his disease he was confined to the house only nine days and to his bed only three. A few days before his departure he said, "O, if I could only preach the blessed Gospel once more to my fellow men, how would my heart rejoice." When he felt that the end was at hand he was perfectly resigned to the Divine will, saying to a brother in the ministry, "I feel now that my work is done; If my good Lord would cut the cord which binds me to earth, how delightfully would I pass away and be at rest. I wish you, my brother, to give my love to the conference, say to the preachers that I still love them; and that the same doctrines preached by me while in health afford me the greatest comfort now when I am about to die." He then exclaimed—

" Jordan's streams shall not o'erflow me,
    While my Saviour's by my side ;
    Canaan, Canaan, lies before me,
        Rise and cross the swelling tide."

This calm faith and hope sustained him to the last. His mind never wandered for an instant. Reason was unwavering, even clear and strong to life's utmost verge, and then his dying testimony is unclouded by even the falling shadow of a momentary delirium. He lingered until past midnight on the morning of Wednesday, December 5th, 1855, so gently that they who watched the scene knew not when his spirit passed away. As a Christian, Brother Talley was devout, earnest and conscientious, publicly and privately, in word and deed. The Gospel of peace was his chief joy and he clung to its blessed truths with a confidence that never wavered. The leading features of his piety were reverence and conscientiousness. As a preacher he did not excel in those qualities which attract the superficial hearer. His sermons were remarkably scriptural, abounding in the very words spoken by the Holy Ghost throughout, and deriving their illustrations principally from the scripture narratives. His knowledge of the Bible indeed was uncommonly full and accurate. In preaching, his range of subjects was not extensive ; Christ the Redeemer, the Holy Spirit, the sanctifier and purifier were his favorite themes ; he led to Christ, to repentance, faith and holiness, nor did he care to tread in speculation beyond what God had revealed.

As a pastor and manager Brother Talley excelled. His work is done and his sun has gone down but not out. It shall come forth again like the star of the morning to shine amid the splendor of an eternal day.— *New Jersey Con. Memorial.*

James Harris

Was admitted on trial in the New Jersey Conference in 1854, and stationed at Frenchtown.

The writer infers from old manuscript now before him that Brother Harris was abundant in labor while on this charge. His next appointment was Westfield, N. J.

We are not able to trace his ministerial record further, as his name drops out of the minutes of the conference.

Wm. M. Burroughs.

Rev. Wm. M. Burroughs was born in Hopewell Township, Mercer County, N. J., June 21st, 1814, and died at New Prospect, N. J., April 17th, 1864. We have but few facts connected with his early life.

REV. GEORGE H. JONES.

(See Page 77)

The event which ultimately shaped his life-work was his conversion, which took place at Pennington in his nineteenth year. Soon after, on the 13th day of October, 1832, he was baptized and received into the M. E. Church on probation, by Rev. Wm. H. Bull, for whom he always cherished a deep affection.

Filled with the love of God and of precious souls, as well as diligent in the use of all the means of grace, it was not long before he was deeply impressed with the conviction that it was his duty to preach the Gospel.

Yielding to the guidance of the Holy Spirit, and in obedience to the call of the Church, he began to preach on Asbury Circuit in 1837, in connection with Rev. Jos. Chattle and C. S. Vancleve.

When the young itinerant left his paternal home to engage in his high vocation, his father gave him a horse, saying: "Go and do all the good you can for I have never done any." His future career shows that he obeyed both the spirit and the letter of that injunction. In 1838, he labored in Newton Circuit in connection with Rev. J. S. Swain. In 1839, he was admitted on trial in the New Jersey Conference. His subsequent appointments were the following: Warren, 1839; Vernon, 1840; Hudson, 1841; Port Jervis, 1842; Milford, Pa., 1843; Ramapo, 1844-'5; Dover, 1846-'7; Bergen, 1848; Rome and Wantage, 1849-'50; Stillwater, 1851-'2; Hope, 1853-'4; Newton, 1855-'6; Frenchtown and Milford, 1857-'8; Kingwood, 1859-'60; Wesley Chapel, 1861; Piermont and Tappen, 1862; New Prospect, 1863 He was just beginning his second year on the last-named charge, when he was called from labor to reward. The last seven years of his life were in connection with the Newark Conference, with which he became identified at the division of the New Jersey Conference. On his return to his charge after the last session of our conference, he entered upon his labors with cheerfulness and hope, but his labors were soon to close.

Suddenly and with great violence he was attacked with congestion of the brain, resulting in apoplexy, which speedily terminated his earthly career.

Thus fell Brother Burroughs in the ripeness of his manhood, having served with fidelity the church to whose ministry he had given himself more than a quarter of a century before.

From the time that he was attacked by the disease, he was unable to speak. He could not give his dying testimony in favor of the religion of Jesus, but he has left to his bereaved family, and to our afflicted Church, the precious testimony of a Christian life.

Our beloved brother needs no eulogy from us. He rests from his labors and his works do follow him. He was a kind husband, an affectionate father, a true friend.

As a pastor he devoted himself earnestly to the welfare of his people, and secured both their respect and affection.

His mental powers were solid rather than brilliant, and his sermons were compact, instructive, and useful.

His discourses near the close of his life are said to have been marked with peculiar unction and power.

He preached with much tenderness not long before his death, on the seventh chapter of Revelation, from the thirteenth to the seventeenth verses, dwelling with rapture on the glories of Heaven, and on the blessedness of those who reach it. Is it wrong to believe that God was leading the mind of his servant to contemplate more and more that blessed home into which he was so soon to enter?

Without bigotry, he was at the same time a firm believer in the distinctive doctrines of Methodism and loved to preach them.

He was a man of even temper, a lover of peace, and a promoter of harmony.

He was one of those rare men whose modesty and reserve prevent the full appreciation of their merits.

Those who knew Brother Burroughs best esteemed him most. Having faithfully done his duty in every position to which the Church assigned him during a ministry of twenty-five years, Brother Burroughs has been gathered to the companionship of those who have turned many to righteousness, leaving a wife and three daughters to the care of the church.

When our work on earth is done may it be said of each one of us, what we can all say of our departed brother: He was a "good Minister of Jesus Christ."—*Newark Con. Minutes.*

George H. Jones

Was received on trial in the New Jersey Conference in 1852, and was sent to Clinton, as junior preacher. In 1853, New Dover and Metuchen; 1854, New Prospect; 1855-'56, Cranbury; 1857-'58, Cokesbury; 1859, Newark City Mission; 1860, Frenchtown; 1861, Harmony; 1862-'63, Vernon and New Milford; 1864, Rockaway.

In 1865, at the annual conference held at Elizabeth, N. J., he was returned as supernumerary, and now resides in Camden, N. J.

REV. JOHN W. BARRETT.

See Page 73

John W. Barrett.

Brother Barrett was born at Camden, N. J., September 20th, 1819. He was admitted on trial in New Jersey Conference in 1843. His appointments were as follows: Clinton circuit, 1843; Rahway, 1844; Hope, 1845; Bergen, 1846; Madison, 1847; Bargainstown, (as junior with W. C. Nelson), 1848-'49; Freehold (as junior preacher), 1850-'51; Perth Amboy, 1852-'53; River Church, 1854-'55; Sharpstown, 1856; Woodbridge, 1857-'58; Frenchtown, 1859; Mendham, 1860; Verona, 1861; Rockaway, 1862-'63; Springfield and Milburn, 1864; North Haverstraw, 1865, and Flora Falls, 1866.

In 1867, he was returned as supernumerary, and is thus marked in the minutes for the next seven years.

In 1875, he is again in the active work with Walpac Center as his field of labor. Broadway, 1876-'77; Centerville and Greenville, N. Y., 1878-'79; Hibernia, 1880; Kingwood, 1881-'82; Mt. Horeb, 1883-'84; Mt. Hope and Tebo, 1885; Hibernia, 1886-'87-'88-'89-'90.

After thirty-eight years of active work in the ministry he was returned supernumerary in 1891, and now resides in Newark, N. J.

Walter Chamberlin.

Brother Chamberlin was born in the Township of Sharon, Litchfield County, Connecticut, April 12th, 1822. His parents were Rufus and Olive Chamberlin. He was converted at the age of twelve, near the place of his birth. Though his parents were members of the M. E. Church, and the good old Bible lay on the stand, and used every morning and night, yet the immediate means of leading him to Christ, in so early a period of his life, was an invitation given him by an elect sister to go to a Methodist altar. The principal part of his education was from a graduating course at Amenia Seminary, Erastus O. Haven, finally Bishop Haven, was principal, Gilbert Haven, also Bishop Haven, was one of the teachers.

He joined the old New Jersey Conference in 1849, and was sent to the Delaware circuit, about thirty miles in extent on the west side of the Delaware. The Master gave him that year 150 souls. 1850-'51, Otisville; 1852-'53, Stanhope; 1854, Palisades; 1855-'56, North Haverstraw; 1857-'58, Boonton; 1859-'60, Springfield; 1861-'62, Frenchtown; 1863-'64, Stillwater and Blairstown; 1865-'66 '67, Perth Amboy; 1869-'70, Spring Valley; 1871-'72, Glen Gardner; 1873-'74, Deckertown and Wantage; 1875-'76'77, Thiells and Garnerville; 1878, Long Branch, First Church; 1879-'80, Vincentown; 1881-'82-'83, Denville;

1884, Raritan; 1885'86-'87, Asbury, thus making thirty-eight consecutive years in the work of the ministry.

W. E. Blakeslee.

The subject of this sketch, Rev. W. E. Blakeslee was born in Orange County, New York, May 19th, 1836. His father, Mr. J. D. Blakeslee, was a mechanic and a man of sterling integrity and well known in the county. His family of nine children were brought up in the fear of God and learned to love righteousness.

In 1851, the father with his family moved to Broome County and settled near Binghampton, where Brother Blakeslee received the principal part of his education, but spent considerable time afterward in a select school at Windsor, under the management of Rev. Rinker, pastor of the Presbyterian Church of that village; being an earnest student he made rapid advancement in his studies, and in 1856 he returned to Orange County and engaged in teaching school. Before returning to Orange County, he united with the M. E. Church at East Windsor, Broome County, when about twenty years of age; he had however, given his heart to God when about twelve years old, largely through the influence of his Christian parents. After teaching one year in Orange County, in November, 1857, he was called by Rev. B. Day, Presiding Elder, of Newton District to supply the pulpit in the church at Vernon, Sussex County, N. J., the health of the pastor having failed. Being young and inexperienced he entered upon his new work with fear and trembling, but fully persuaded that God had called him to the work of the Christian ministry. Here God wonderfully blessed his labors, and during these four months before conference, seventy souls were converted and brought into the church; this settled his life-work. In the spring of 1858, he united with the Newark Conference at its first session held in Morristown. Some of the members of the class joining at that time have become noted men. Bishop John F. Hirst, H. A. Butts, D. D., S. L. Baldwin, D. D., and Sylvester Opdyke and A. Craig, who served successfully as Presiding Elder, were members of his class.

Brother Blakeslee has served the following charges within the bounds of the Newark Conference: Vernon, Oakland and Forestburg, Bloomsbury and Finesville, Milford and Little York, Frenchtown and Everittstown, Sparta, Lafayette, Tranquility, Andover, Rockaway, Wesley Church, Phillipsburg; Port Jervis; Eighth avenue, Newark; Linden avenue, Jersey City; First Church, Dover; Perth Amboy, and is now serving Fulton Street Church, in the city of Elizabeth.

REV. WALTER CHAMBERLIN.

(See Page 86.)

In 1860, during his pastorate at Bloomsbury, he was united in marriage to Miss Charlotte R. Brown, of Broome County, N. Y., who was a student with him at the school in Windsor in 1856. During these years of his ministry she has shared with him his toils and his triumphs. He has not only enjoyed extensive revivals during his ministry, but has built one church and laid the foundation of three others; has built also three parsonages and did a good deal of hard work in raising money to remove cumbersome debts from the church property in his various charges. His pastorate at Frenchtown was one upon which he looks back with a good deal of pleasure. Though it occurred during the dark days of war and strife, still harmony prevailed in the church, the congregation remained large and souls were converted who remain till the present time as witnesses to the power of Christ to save.

Friendships were then formed that will be as lasting as eternity, and when the final harvest shall be gathered, sheaves from Frenchtown will be brought in to tell of earnest toil and honest labor for the Master.

Henry J. Hayter.

Henry J. Hayter was converted at the altar in the Somerville M. E. Church, at the age of eighteen years, under the ministry of Rev. R. B. Yard, November 22d, 1851, and connected himself the next morning (Sabbath) with the church. He was licensed to preach in 1854, by the Union Street Quarterly Conference, Newark, N. J. He was placed in charge of the South Orange Church by the Presiding Elder, Thomas McCarroll, in 1855. In 1856 he was received into the Annual Conference and appointed to Basking Ridge and Bernardsville as junior preacher. He was sent to Frenchtown in 1865, remaining three years.

God was very graciously with him, and he had a revival each year, and the converts received, added greatly to the working force of the church. Milford was attached to Frenchtown the third year, and seventy souls were converted. From that revival four young men went out to preach the Gospel, one of them, Nomer J. Wright, of the New Jersey Conference, is doing noble work for Christ and Methodism. Bro. Hayter writes: "We had a noble band of Methodists at Frenchtown. They were true to God, true to Methodism, and true to their country." Many of them have gone to their glorious reward, among them the ever faithful Morris Maxwell, and the brave soldier Johnson J. Lair, and Obadiah Stout, who also shouldered his rifle and fought bravely for the Union, came back without a stain upon his character and took his honored place in the church. A few days after my appointment at Frenchtown, Gen. Lee surrendered. The whole town was alive with joy. At night every street was bright with the illuminated windows. But oh! alas, alas! how soon came the sad, sad tidings of the assassination of the immortal Lincoln. We fell from our highest joy to our deepest grief; where could we go but to God. The different congregations met on April 19th in the Baptist Church, to join in services appropriate to the funeral of our beloved martyred President; the pastors of the Baptist, Presbyterian and Methodist churches leading in the service.

June 1st was the day appointed by President Johnson as a day of humiliation and prayer. The citizens of the town met in the Presbyterian Church, and I was requested to preach the funeral sermon. My text was, Psalms 50: 15. Call upon me in the day of trouble; I will deliver thee, and thou shalt glorify me.

REV. W. E. BLAKESLEE.

(See Page 76.)

CHAPTER VI.

BRIEF PERSONAL SKETCHES OF THE PASTORS WHO HAVE SERVED
THE FRENCHTOWN M. E. CHURCH—CONTINUED.

"'Tis not a cause of small import
  The pastor's care demands,
  But what might fill an angel's heart,
  And filled a Saviour's hands."

John B. Taylor.

JOHN B. TAYLOR is an earnest and efficient worker in the Master's cause. His three years spent in Frenchtown were full of activities and crowned with the best of results. His pulpit ministrations were both interesting and edifying. Brother Taylor was admitted to the Newark Conference in the spring of 1865. The following is a list of his appointments: Bernardsville, Bloomsbury, Frenchtown, Pine Brook, Clinton, Trinity Church, Staten Island; Boonton, Tottenville, Waverly Church, Jersey City; Hackensack, Bound Brook, Palisades, Jersey City, Port Jervis, Nyack. He has filled some of the best appointments in the Newark Conference.

C. Clark, Jr.

C. Clark, Jr., the subject of this sketch was born in the town of Orange, N. J., February 9th, 1834; he was a son of William H., and Mary Jane Clark. When he was four years old the family moved into Monmouth County, N. J., and settled near Keyport, which was a community of very decided and vigorous Methodists. In this county Mr. Clark spent his boyhood, attending the public schools with regularity, summer and winter, and for two years a private school of higher grade at Keyport, wherein he taught subsequently as assistant principal, for one year previous to entering the ministry. At the age of seventeen, while engaged in a country store as clerk, young Clark began the work of seeking the Lord's favor at a revival held near Navesink under the ministry of Rev. Samuel Morrell, of New Jersey Conference, but before his realizing the regeneration wrought by the Holy Ghost, was necessarily moved to Freehold circuit, where his father was for the year junior preacher, and holding revival meetings in Jackson township, Ocean County, young Clark was very soundly converted to God. He spent subsequently four years in the town of Freehold as a merchant's clerk and as a member of the Methodist Church in that town. About this time in his twenty-first year he was thoroughly aroused by what to him then, was an awful fact, that he was called to enter the ministry of his church and make that his life profession. At first it was an appalling weight on the mind of the young man, who seemed in his own estimation so little qualified for so great a work. For awhile he was disposed to rebel against what seemed to him a Divine call.

At the solicitation of the church and of his faithful pastor, Rev. John Scarlett, he took work in the ministry under the Presiding Elder, Rev. John S. Porter, and in 1856 was stationed at South Orange, N. J. In the spring of 1857, he was received into the traveling ministry at New Jersey Conference session in Greene street, Trenton. His subsequent fields of labor have been, Chatham, Parsippany, Rockaway, Succasunna, Vienna, Hope, Mt. Hope, Frenchtown, Bernardsville, Tottenville and Mariners Harbor, S. I.; Quakertown, N. J.; Thiells and Stony Point, N. Y.; Milford, Pa., and now again Rockaway, N. J., where he is closing up his fourth year, making in all forty years in the ministry. How successful has been his work under God, eternity alone will reveal. In his ministry from the first, revivals of religion have occurred and many of them quite phenominal for influence and number of converts. None more than the one occurring in Frenchtown on the third year of his residence there, when it did seem as if Pentecost and the Saul of Tarsus conversions, and the scene of the Philippian jail were almost reproduced.

We will add, his three years of labor here were fraught with blessed results as far reaching as eternity. May he at last hear the "well done," "thou hast been faithful over a few things, I will make thee ruler over many things; enter thou into the joy of thy Lord."

Hamilton C. McBride

Was admitted into the Philadelphia Conference in 1866, and stationed at Garrettstown, 1867, Portland, Pa.

In 1868, he entered the Newark Conference and served Centenary Church, Jersey City, for two years. In 1870, his appointment was Irvington, and in 1871 (assistant pastor), Central Church, Newark. In 1872-'73, Bernardsville; 1874, Frenchtown.

In 1875, at the session of the Newark Conference, held in Trinity Church, Jersey City, he was granted a supernumerary relation, and is now engaged in evangelistic werk.

REV. HENRY J. HAYTER.

(See Page 79.)

Edward Morrell Griffith.

Was born at Elizabethtown, N. J., March 5th, 1822, and died at Hilton, N. J., May 23d, 1884. He was connected with some of the best families in New Jersey Methodism—Methodist of the Methodists for four generations. His great-grandfather, Robert Duncan, was converted under the preaching of John Wesley, and when he came to America during the Revolution, he united with old John Street Church, New York. Bro. Griffith's parents were earnest Christians. His father was a native of Wales, and his mother was born in South Norwalk, Conn. Our brother was converted in South Norwalk in February, 1833, under the ministry of Rev. A. F. Francis. "Of my conversion," said he, "I never had the shadow of a doubt." Rev. D. W. Bartine, D.D., gave him his license as Exhorter at Morristown, N. J., in 1841, and he was licensed to preach by the Burlington Quarterly Conference in 1843. The following year he was admitted to the New Jersey Conference, and was stationed at Tom's River- a circuit which comprised nearly the whole of what is now Ocean County, and which required four weeks to fill the round of appointments.

As he was the junior preacher and unmarried, he was expected to keep in motion; consequently he had no boarding place and tarried only a night. But the Lord was with him, and a remarkable revival at Crammertown rewarded his labor. In 1845 he was sent as colleague with Rev. James Long on the Tuckerton circuit, which, like that of Tom's River, was thirty-five miles in length. Here again the Lord was gracious and visited his people. In 1846 he was appointed to Columbus circuit, with six places to preach. The next two years he ministered at Mendham and Bernardsville, and revivals broke out in both places. He was married, March 7th, 1849, to Miss Marietta Kitchell, of Morristown, and the union proved a very happy one. This estimable lady survives him.

During 1849-'50 he was stationed at Caldwell; 1851-'52, at Dover; 1853-'54, at Middletown Point; 1855, at Heightstown; 1856-'57, at Belvidere. In the spring of 1858, when the New Jersey Conference was divided, his lot was cast with the Newark Conference, and he was pastor at Vienna during the next two years. In 1860 he preached at Rockland Lake, N. Y., and then, on account of broken health, he was on the supernumerary list until the spring of 1867, when he was stationed at Peapack. After this he filled the following appointments: 1868-'69, Somerville; 1870-71, Woodbridge; 1872-'74, Woodrow, Staten Island; 1875-'76, Frenchtown. Subsequently he removed to Hilton, near Newark, where he resided until his death.

From 1877 until the close of his life he had no regular charge, as the precarious state of his health would not admit of it; but he preached frequently when strength seemed to be returning; and his friends were hoping that he would soon be restored to his former vigor and hold up again the Lamp of Life to dying men. But heart disease and a general relaxation of the physical powers gave warning that the end was drawing near. Four years ago we thought he was sinking to the grave; and I shall never forget the words he whispered to me, for his voice was nearly gone: "Never cease to preach the Gospel, brother; never do anything else, no matter how poorly you fare." "Tell the preachers I love them. Tell my brethren not to turn aside from the preaching of the Gospel. Tell them to preach neither for honor nor applause, but for the glory of God. It is a glorious work. I die in the faith which I espoused at eleven years of age, and which I have preached for so many years. I do not pride myself on anything I have done. My trust is in Christ. He is my life and my light. I am not in the dark!" Though his eyes were closed in weariness and the tears were on the good man's face, a certain radiance rested there that showed how true was every word that he had spoken.

I have heard him say more than once, "Oh, I love to preach the Gospel!" It was no common favor to be the intimate friend of such a man. Very few people knew him well. Naturally retiring, he was nevertheless one of the most companionable of men when in congenial company. His tastes were literary. He contributed many valuable historical articles to the columns of the *Christian Advocate*. One large manuscript volume, comprising an exhaustive history of *Methodism in Warren County* and other portions of northern New Jersey, is the careful work of his facile pen.

A few weeks before he died I visited him, and he placed in my hands the manuscript of a volume which he had penned within the last year of his life, entitled: "The Land of Beulah." As he said, it was written among the shadows of death. It is full of most vigorous thought, and is a development of the doctrine of the supremacy of the spiritual over the natural. It need scarcely be told that the *tone* of the work is full of sweet religiousness.

We all remember the effect of Brother Griffith's letter, read to the conference of 1883—how all hearts were thrilled in the large audience as the words were heard which told of an unspeakable joy in the midst of a wasting disease. Brother Griffith was a student. His sermons were carefully prepared, and, in the days of his strength, were delivered with energy and effect. They were logical. That was their prime characteristic, though they were not wanting in

REV. J. B. TAYLOR.

(See Page 8

other qualities when occasion called them forth. Whatever of pathos there might be in his preaching was rather the pathos of earnestness. Revivals of religions were not uncommon in the charges where he ministered, and many souls were converted through his efforts. But his great work as a preacher was in the edification of believers and the establishing of the church in the faith; and it is not too much to say that in this department of Christian labor he was abundantly successful. Blessed in the companionship of a devoted wife, two daughters and a son, his last days were full of comforting kindness and spent in cheerful expectation of that entering into rest of which he held the promise.

In our last interview he spoke of his trust in Christ and the great peace that filled his soul. He was very feeble in body, but his mental vigor was astonishing. His thoughts upon holy themes, and we talked of little else, were expressed with a force and unction which mated strangely with the distressing cough which punctuated his glowing sentences. He said that many times when the hours of sleeplessness would have been heavy with watching for the morning, his heart would be filled with the goodness of the Lord, and eyes and soul would overflow together in joyful thanksgiving.

Among his papers was found one, evidently written but a short time before he died, with the word " Jesus " on the margin; and it reads: " I wish here to record one fact, and impress it upon the memory of all my children, of my dear wife, and of all my friends; *Jesus is my unfailing friend.* I relinquish you all and I hold on to Him. *I know* Him. I have been very unfaithful, but He does not cast me off. I have to Him given soul and body. Think of your husband, your father, your brother—my wife, my children, my sisters—as now with the Lord. Give your hearts to Jesus and come to me beyond the Gates of Pearl!"

The funeral was held in the Irvington Church, under the direction of Presiding Elder Brice. Revs. J. F. Andrew, T. T. Campfield, Dr. E. H. Stokes, A. E. Ballard, George Hughes, W. G. Wiggins, J. P. Fort, and the writer, participated in the service. We buried him in Fairmount Cemetery, Newark, among the ashes of his kindred; and God has marked the place where he sleeps.—*Newark Con. Minutes.*

P. G. Ruckman

Was admitted into the Newark Conference in 1870, and was sent to Sparrowbush as his first field of labor. His subsequent appointments were: Centerville and Greenville, N. Y.; New City, N. Y.; Sergeantsville, N. J.

At the annual conference in 1875, he was granted a supernumerary relation; Rev. E. M. Griffith's health failing, Brother Ruckman was sent by the Elder to Frenchtown, to fill out the balance of the year.

His labors were abundantly blessed, a gracious revival of religion was the result, and the fruit remains unto this day.

The following year he went West, and took work in the Nebraska Conference, where he labored successfully for seven years. He returned to the Newark Conference in 1891, and was appointed to Buttzville charge, serving three years.

At the next conference session, convened in Centenary Church, Jersey City, he was transferred to the Wyoming Conference.

Rev. James H. Runyan.

James Henry Runyan was born at Liberty Corners, Somerset County, N. J., August 28th, 1833, and died at Bethel, Staten Island, January 19th, 1888.

When four years of age his parents moved to Bayonne, Hudson County, N. J.; here he spent six years of his boyhood in the schools. When he reached the age of ten his parents again moved to Staten Island, N. Y., where he lived until about seventeen years of age, in the meantime receiving such education as the schools could afford. From Staten Island he went to Newark to learn the trade of silversmith, and while at his trade the spirit of the Lord found him out, and he at once turned his face Godward and earnestly sought and found Christ in the pardon of his sins, at a watch-night service in the Halsey Street Church, 1852, being then about nineteen years of age. His conversion was clear and positive, and he began at once to work for the Master, distributing tracts and books throughout the city, and going to the outposts to assist in holding meetings, at the same time devoting his leisure moments to the study of such books as he could obtain by his own labor, and receiving some assistance from his father. His gifts and graces soon attracted the attention of the church, and he was licensed to exhort by the Union Street Quarterly Conference, March 1st, 1854, Richard Vanhorne, pastor. In 1855 he was called to supply Buttzville and Harmony circuit, and licensed to preach by Buttzville Quarterly Conference, M. Force, P. E. In the spring of 1856 he was admitted to the ministry in the New Jersey Conference, and appointed to Montague, N. J. His subsequent appointments were: 1857, Delaware, Pa.; 1858, Marshall's Creek, Pa.; 1859-'60, Narrowsburgh, N. Y.; 1861-'62, West Milford, N. J.; 1863-'64, Rome and Greenville, N. J.; 1865-'66, Stillwater and Swartswood, N. J.; 1867-'68, Branchville

REV. C. CLARK, JR.

(See Page 8.)

and Frankford Pl., N. J.; 1869, Cokesbury, N. J.; 1870-'71, Vienna and Janes Chapel, N. J.; 1872-'73-'74, Succasunna, N. J.; 1875-'76, Peapack and Chester, N. J.; 1877-'78-'79, Frenchtown, N. J.; 1880-'81-'82, Linden avenue, Jersey City, N. J.; 1883-'84-'85, Woodbridge, N. J.; 1886-'87, Bethel, Staten Island, N. Y., where he ceased at once to work and live. On March 31st, 1859, he was united in marriage to Miss Marilla Shay, who for twenty-eight years shared with him the joys and sorrows of the itinerancy. To them five children were born, two of whom have died, while one son and two daughters live to claim our sympathy and prayers.

Brother Runyan was ordained deacon April 4th, 1858, by Bishop E. R. Ames, and ordained elder April 8th, 1860, by Bishop Levi Scott. His ministry was one of extensive usefulness. Revival work was his delight, his greatest joy was in seeing sinners coming to God. He was a bold champion of the truth. When it cost something to be something, he was willing to pay the price. When the war cloud hung over the nation, it cost something to be loyal in those regions where he was called to labor, but he had a loyal heart, and said, cost what it may I shall stand by my country's flag. So in the war against the rum traffic. This principle of fidelity to duty was the key note that gave him inspiration. More than once was he called to pay the price for his loyalty to his country and to God. He was a real man and had no sympathy with shams; to him religion was a reality, not a mere sentiment. He was fearless in his attacks upon sin, and faltered not to attack it in high or low places. He was a good preacher, clear and practical, a faithful expounder of the Word of Life. His aim was to reach the heart rather than the head, yet he failed not to instruct as well as to move to tears those who sat under his ministry. As a man he was genial, always full of good cheer, having a great warm heart that made one feel at home in his presence. As a worker there were few among his brethren more successful. Bethel stands to-day as a monument of his untiring zeal.

His will was indomitable, few, if any, ever made a more heroic fight for life; he stood at his post as a faithful watchman to the last, saying, "I must preach Jesus to the people." Only two weeks before his release, being unable to stand, he sat and preached from 1 Cor. 15: 41, 42: "There is one glory of the sun, and another glory of the moon, and another glory of the stars, for one star differeth from another star in glory. So also is the resurrection of the dead. It is sown in corruption, it is raised in incorruption." This was his last sermon, and the corruption has put on incorruption, "the mortal is clothed with immortality." His funeral services were held in Bethel Methodist Episcopal Church, January 23d, 1888. Addresses were made by Revs. J. N. FitzGerald, S. Van Benschoten, and the writer, about thirty-two of the members of the Conference being in attendance. His remains were laid to rest in a beautiful plot donated by the church in Bethel cemetery. We, with wife and children, revere his memory and mourn his loss. All shall meet in the morning.

> "The grass grows green upon his tomb,
> And flowers bloom above him ;
> Yet still his spirit hovers o'er,
> The dear ones left, who loved him."

Newark Con. Minutes.

Thomas E. Gordon.

Thomas E. Gordon is a preacher perhaps above the average, but not always appreciated for all he is worth. God's workmen chosen to carry on his work, and sent forth to disciple all nations were not all of the same temperament. There was the impulsive Peter, the loving John, etc.

He was admitted to the Newark Conference in 1859. The following is a list of his appointments; Chatham, Greenville, Hudson City, Passaic, Piermont, Otisville, Stillwater and Swartswood, Mt. Horeb, Prospect Street, Paterson; Rockland Lake, Flemington, Quakertown, Frenchtown, Rahway, Tottenville, Bernardsville, Phillipsburg and Harrison, where he is now serving his third year.

He was born in Ireland, trained for a teacher in the Wesleyan Model School, in Dublin, and came to America in 1859.

I. N. Vansant.

Bro. Vansant was born in Atlantic County, N. J., in the year 1830. His father was Nicholas Vansant, who for many years was a devout local preacher. The subject of this sketch was converted when about fourteen years old through the influence of his brother Samuel, who went to his heavenly home a few years ago.

He traveled for some years under the Elder, his first charge as junior preacher being Tuckerton circuit with Abraham Gearhart as preacher, in charge. He next traveled Barnegat circuit one year, then Columbia, and Hainsburg was favored by having him as pastor for two years.

After admission in the Newark Conference, in 1859, he filled the following appointments, viz.: Hope, Stillwater, Wantage, each two

REV. HAMILTON C. McBRIDE.

(See Page 81.)

years. Tranquility, Perth Amboy, Bethel, S. I., each three years, and Clinton, N. J., two years. His next field of labor was Pine Brook, where he remained three years, then he next served East Newark two years, and Stanton and Allerton one year. His next field of labor was Frenchtown, where he remained three years, and his influence there is still a benediction. His next appointment was St. Mark's, S. I., three years, then up the Hudson River to Stony Point, where he remained four years. Quakertown was then favored by having him as pastor for three years, and now he is at Bloomsbury on his first year. Brother Vansant has one son in the ministry.

S. D. Decker.

Brother Decker was born September 11th, 1838, near New Springville, Staten Island, on the old Asbury circuit. His parents were, T. Drummond and Susan Wood Decker. His father was for a number of years class-leader and licensed exhorter, and both were members of the Methodist Episcopal Church for more than forty years, indeed his ancestors for more than a hundred years have been devout Methodists, and he cannot remember a time even from his earliest childhood that he was free from religious convictions. At the age of thirteen, after enduring for several days the most pungent conviction of sin by the Holy Spirit, he came into the noon-day splendor of a clear and positive sense of pardon, and full salvation through faith in Jesus Christ, and has retained until this day the assurance and joy of an indwelling Holy Ghost; not only a Blessing, but the Blesser, Himself.

His now sainted mother and translated father had more to do in leading him to the Saviour and forming his character as a religious boy and Christian man than any other human instrumentality.

Rev. Bartholomew Weed, of precious memory, was at that time pastor on the Asbury charge, Staten Island, for the first time. He served the charge after a few years for a second term.

Brother Decker began his education in the district school of his native village, and has been a reader in general literature and theology for near forty years. After a few years as a licensed exhorter and local preacher, he entered the ranks of the traveling ministry in 1870. His first appointment was East Millstone, in Somerset County, N. J., where he remained two years. Thereafter serving the following charges in the order named: Denville and Rockaway Valley, three years. Here a commodious parsonage was built, the charge never having owned, but rented a house for their pastor. Asbury and Bethlehem in Warren County, two years; New Germantown and Fairmount, two years;

Bloomsbury and Finesville, three years; Clinton, three years; French-town, three years; High Bridge and Lebanon, three years. At the end of his term of service here, Lebanon was taken from High Bridge and connected with Clinton and he went to Clinton for a second term, remaining two years, when Lebanon was made an independent charge. Grace Church, Dover, was the next field of labor where he stayed one year; Deckertown, in Sussex County was his appointment in April, 1894, and he is now on his second year.

In all of these charges, and in every year of service, souls have been converted and added to the church, and in some of them remarkable revivals of religion have occurred, notably, Asbury and Bethlehem, New Germantown and Fairmount, where hundreds of souls were saved and added to the church.

Much time and attention in these various charges were given to the payment of church and parsonage debts, the building of new par-sonages, remodeling and enlarging old ones, and the renovating of churches.

In closing this sketch the writer will add, that Brother Decker's three years in Frenchtown were crowded with Christian activities and crowned with the blessing of the Master.

John O. Winner.

John O. Winner, the subject of this sketch came from a good old Methodist family. The writer remembers hearing his honored father preach more than fifty years ago, and it was he that preached the dedicatorial sermon of this church, December 17th, 1845. John O. Winner was a preacher of more than ordinary ability, of a high intellectual order, and the thoughtful heard him gladly, but he did not succeed in attracting and holding the multitude. The writer sat under his ministry for two years, and the preached word to him was always bread and never a stone.

He has served the following appointments, viz:—1848, Warren circuit; 1849-'50, Rockland; 1851-'52, Quary street, Newark; 1853, Dover; 1854-'55, Plainfield; 1856-'57, Elizabeth; 1858-'59, Prospect street, Paterson; 1860-'61, Hudson City; 1862-'63, Hoboken; 1864, Trinity, S. I. For the next seven years he was returned as super-numerary. He again took up the active work in 1873, Mt. Zion was the appointment; 1874-'75-'76, Millstone; 1877, Plainfield, with Brother Day; 1878, Hope; 1879-'80, Tranquility; 1881, Tranquility and Johnsonborough; 1882-'83, Belvidere; 1884, Passaic; 1885-'86-'87, Bloomsbury; 1888-'89, Frenchtown; 1890-'91-'92-'93, Woodrow, S. I.;

REV. E. M. GRIFFITH.
(See Page 87.)

1891, Alpine. At the last session of the Newark Conference held at Tottenville, N. Y., at his request, he was granted a supernumerary relation, and now resides near Pennington, N. J. He has a son in the ministry now stationed at Somerville.

Morris T. Gibbs.

Morris T. Gibbs was born in Warren County, N. J., about forty years ago. He has been in the active work of the ministry fifteen years, two of which were spent in connection with the M. E. Church of Frenchtown. As a child, he was modest and retiring, but diligent in school work, standing among his fellows well up toward the head of his class. He gave his heart to God when quite young, and concluding that religion meant service he immediately set himself to carry out the Divine command, "Go work to-day in my vineyard." His early Christian life was prophetic of what came later. Method and industry were prominent traits of character; not the sky-rocket brilliancy type, but a gentle, even, pushing forward, with zealous determination to secure its object, and seldom failing to do it. Naturally affable and kind, these qualities became polished and beautified by companionship with Jesus. In the conference minutes of 1880, under the disciplinary question, who are admitted on trial, occurs the name of the subject of this biography. His first appointment was not St. Paul's, of Newark, or the wealthy Cobb Memorial Church, of Morristown, but a modest little church containing a few earnest Christians on the Delaware, a few miles below Milford, called Dingman's Ferry, where he received three hundred and thirty-two dollars in compensation for the first year's service. He remained on this charge for two years, when he left this paradise of summer boarders for the inviting hills of Sussex County, and settled for two years at Branchville. Paterson and Rockaway are successively favored with his service, each place retaining him for three years. From Rockaway he came to Frenchtown, where the people found in him an earnest Christian worker, full of faith and zeal, a steadfast friend of every good cause. This is his commendation, the people were glad when he came among them, sorry when at the expiration of two years he went away. The Frenchtown M. E. Church has had a number of excellent pastors, but none of them have done better work on the charge than the Rev. Morris T. Gibbs.

William McCain.

William McCain was born at Mt. Hermon, Warren County, N. J., August 11th, 1840. He is the son of Jeremiah and Amelia McCain.

In his father's family there were six children, four sons and two daughters. The death of his mother in her seventy-sixth year was the first to break the family circle. At this writing, his father in his eightieth year, in good health, resides on the farm, where he was born, and where all of his children were brought up. The subject of this sketch was converted in his thirteenth year, immediately after a brief season of severe sickness. At this period his mind was turned to the reading of the Bible and religious books, contributing by way of preparation to his future calling. As he approached manhood, worldliness and business interests interfered in degree at least with the Divine plan.

In his twenty-fourth year he openly gave himself anew to God, and received by way of renewal the clear and joyful witness of the Spirit. At different times following this he was further led into the glorious experience of Scriptural Holiness or perfect love. Soon after his renewal in Christ, or conversion, he was clearly called to preach the Gospel. This call he resisted for several years, and it was only at the eleventh hour in order to secure peace of mind and save his own soul that he yielded to the Divine command. His studies, beyond a common school education were largely secured in a private way in the home, with the exception of a brief period at Pennington Seminary. The conference course of study laid down in the discipline was all carefully gone over with notes before entering the ministry.

The appointments he has filled in the Newark Conference are as follows: Libertyville and Coleville, 1872-'73; Branchville and Frankford Plains, 1874-'75-'76; Milford, Pa., 1877-'78-'79; Andover, 1880-'81-'82; Lafayette, 1883; Little Falls, 1884-'85-'86; Succasunna, 1887-'88-'89; Rockaway, 1890-'91; Frenchtown, 1892-'93-'94; Clinton, 1895. In this latter appointment he is now laboring, exceedingly happy that God ever counted him faithful by putting him in the ministry. He was united in marriage, January 31st, 1877, to Elizabeth J. Dimon, daughter of J. N. V. and Julia Dimon, of Branchville, N. J. The children born to them are Julia B., Maggie A., and Willie H. Maggie A. was early called to her heavenly home.

E. H. Conklin.

The present pastor of the church, the Rev. Elkanah H. Conklin, was born in the State of New York, Huntington, Long Island, October 1st, 1846. He has no recollection of his father, as he died when he was quite young. His mother, with three brothers, two sisters and their father, came to this country from England in the early years of the present century. She was a member of the Episcopal Church, and

REV. JAMES H. RUNYAN.

(See Page 92.)

earnestly desired that all her children should be confirmed in the same faith ; with reference to our subject, however, she died without having her wish gratified ; but her prayers were not in vain for he was converted to God and joined the Methodist Episcopal Church in the year 1865, at the age of nineteen. These years were filled with mystery, sorrow and sin. A prolonged battle with three giants, Ignorance, Poverty and Evil. From the dawn of consciousness his was a wilderness experience. His boyhood seems, as he looks back upon it, a troubled dream, and he has never had any sympathy with the commonly expressed desire, "I would I were a boy again." His conversion was a double exodus ; a going out of himself and his native land ; a veritable passage of the Jordan, with Egypt and the wilderness left behind forever, and the Land of Promise pressed by angel feet and rendered heavenly by angelic songs, and sanctified by the Holy Prophets and the Divine Christ, henceforth became his abiding place. He was led to Christ by the personal solicitation of a fellow workman whose simple words ; "Don't you think you ought to be a Christian ?" went to his heart like an arrow.

In 1867, he united with St. Paul's Church, Jersey City, where he became associated with an earnest band of young Christians, among whom he found a field for the operation of all his youthful enthusiasm. Here he first received the impression from which he could never rid himself, that he ought to devote his life to the work of the ministry. This call to preach the Gospel found him with a double impoverishment of intellect and pocket, and while he felt deeply that he ought to preach, he felt no less deeply the need of mental preparation for the work. The one conviction was no stronger than the other He had obtained salvation without money and without price, but education could not be obtained without dollars and plenty of hard work. The way to the Cross had been easy, but the way to the school was filled with hindrances that made it as impenetrable as the walls of Jericho, but it will be remembered that the walls of this ancient city fell flat before the march of prayer and faith, and so this spiritual force opened the way to six consecutive years of school training. There seemed to be only one person who could render this needed assistance. His name was Henry Halsey, a shipping merchant, an uncle by marriage on his mother's side. He was a worldly man and could hardly be expected to aid a young man preparing for the ministry. After a season of prayer in his behalf, he paid him a visit, told his religious experience, and was about to solicit a loan, when to his surprise the uncle said: "And now you want to attend school to prepare for the ministry, and

want me to help you, do you? Very well, go ahead, send me the bills,
I will pay them," and this he continued to do for two years when he
suddenly died. During the next four years his school expenses were
met by teaching, preaching and canvassing for books during the summer vacation. He graduated from Pennington Seminary in 1870, and
from Dickinson College in 1874. The same year he united with the
Newark Conference at its annual session in Paterson, N. J.

He has served the following churches: Midland Park, Otisville,
Metuchen, Millbrook, St. Paul's, Newark; Rockaway, Blairstown,
Deckertown, Englewood, Calvary Church, Paterson; Somerville, and
is now serving his first year at Frenchtown.

David Curtis.

Brother Curtis was born near Baptistown, Hunterdon County, N. J.,
in 1823, and died in Holland Township, near Milford, December 10th,
1887. A widow and eight children survive him.

He was converted in early life, at Lambertville, under the ministry
of Rev. A. E. Ballard, and connected himself with the M. E. Church
at that place; but at the time of his death was connected with the
Frenchtown M. E. Church. He received a local preacher's license from
the Frenchtown Quarterly Conference, August 22d, 1884, and in 1887
was sent by the Presiding Elder as junior preacher to Sergeantsville
and Stockton circuit to fill out part of a year.

Brother Curtis did not have the advantages of a college education,
but was well versed in general literature, and was a man of good
natural ability. At the time of his death he was a member of Orion
Lodge, F. and A. M., Manhattan Tribe, I. O. R. M., and of the Odd
Fellows, also of the Delaware Encampment, of Patriarchs, No. 11.

As a preacher he was well received, and while not brilliant, yet it
may be said of him as it was of Stephen, "He was full of faith and
the Holy Ghost."

Lewis J. Gordon.

Lewis J. Gordon was born in Milford, Hunterdon County, N. J.,
February 17th, 1859. He is engaged in business in Frenchtown, where
he now resides.

He was converted at the age of twelve, under the pastorate of Bro.
John B. Taylor, in the Methodist Church at Frenchtown, and united
with the same in 1871. Like many others of his age he forgot to
" watch and pray," but was reclaimed during the pastorate of Rev.

Rev. Thomas E. Gordon.

(See Page 86.)

Thomas E. Gordon, and received a special blessing of Christian liberty under the pastorate of Rev. I. N. Vansant.

He received a local preacher's license at the third quarterly conference of the Frenchtown M. E. Church, February 10th, 1888. He is an acceptable preacher and an efficient worker in the evangelistic field of labor, and has successfully conducted meetings in Delaware, Pennsylvania and New York.

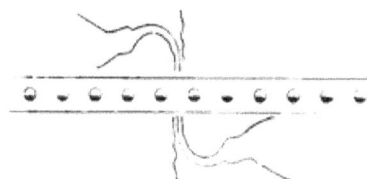

8*

CHAPTER VII.

THE PART THE FRENCHTOWN M. E. CHURCH BORE IN SUPPRESSING THE REBELLION.

BY WILLIAM T. SKOPE.

"IT is no fault in others that the Methodist Church sends more soldiers to the field, more nurses to the hospitals, and more prayers to Heaven than any other. God bless the Methodist Church! Bless all the churches, and blessed be God, who in this our great trial, giveth us the churches.   ABRAHAM LINCOLN."

In response to a call made by the government at Washington for more soldiers to put down the Rebellion, a public meeting was held at Frenchtown, July 22d, 1862, to render all assistance possible to suppress treason and secession, and restore the union of the States.

William H. Slater, a prominent merchant and hardware dealer of the town, was present at this meeting and stated that he had enlisted in the service of his country, and called upon all patriots present to come forward and do likewise.

Many responded, and Mr. Slater was chosen Captain of Company G, Fifteenth Regiment, New Jersey Volunteers, and was duly commissioned as such, August 15th, 1862.

Many members of this, and other companies were then, or have been since, either directly connected with the M. E. Church of Frenchtown, or among its supporters and contributors; and it is of these persons, heroes we may say, that we purpose now to allude briefly to in this chapter.

How well do we remember when the "boys" left for the tented field and the hardships of war! We recall those sad parting scenes as vividly now as when they happened. We can hear the choked farewell, the sob, the sigh, as wives, fathers, mothers, sisters, brothers and sweethearts were embraced in many instances for the last time! One young man, with tears in his eyes, said to us as he stepped aboard the train, "my hardest battle was parting with my wife!" But we shall not dwell upon scenes of this character, but rather upon the brief individual sketches which we have been asked to produce.

REV. I. N. VANSANT.

(see Page 96)

The service of Captain Slater was of short duration. At the first battle of Fredericksburg, December 13th, 1862, he was so badly wounded in the right leg, that amputation was absolutely necessary. Yet despite the awful suffering he underwent in the loss of so important a member as a leg, he is alive to-day and resides in Washington City.

Agustus Cronce

Was born in the Township of Clinton, Hunterdon County, N. J., March 5th, 1834.

He learned the trade of cabinetmaker with Henry Bachman, of Frenchtown.

He was a member of Company G, Fifteenth Regiment, enlisting August 14th, 1862. On June 4th, 1864, he was struck in the arm by a bullet fired by a rebel picket, shattering the member so badly that the surgeon was compelled to amputate it. The same bullet passed through the cap of Samuel Hoff, now residing at Everittstown, who stood less than three feet from Mr. Cronce. It then passed so closely to the neck of William H. Cawley, now of Somerville, that a mark was made upon the skin.

Mr. Cronce was discharged from service, May 1st, 1865, and since the close of the war has lived retired in Frenchtown.

Horace A. Wambaugh,

A son of Mahlon and Elizabeth Wambaugh, was enrolled in Company D, Thirtieth Regiment, New Jersey Volunteers, September 3d, 1862, and was discharged for disability, February 23d, 1863.

He was a farmer by occupation, and resided several years on the farm now owned by Catharine Rittenhouse, on the road leading from Frenchtown to Baptisttown. He now resides at Trenton with his son.

Simon A. Eisenhart

Was born in Lehigh County, Pennsylvania, May 13th, 1838, and was married to Wilhemina Vanluvance, May 30th, 1867, and has one son and two daughters.

He was enrolled in Company M, Colonel Coman's Mounted Rifle Rangers, afterwards known as the Eighth Pennsylvania Cavalry, September 28th, 1861.

He was in several battles, and was wounded in the right foot, June 24th, 1864, which was amputated.

He was discharged from the service September 28th, 1864.

He is a shoemaker by trade, but is now following the business of florist, at Erwinna, Bucks County, Pennsylvania.

Demerest Gordon,

A son of William Gordon and Henrietta Volk, was born October 2d, 1844.

He was enrolled in Company D, Thirtieth Regiment, New Jersey Volunteers, September 3d, 1862, as musician, and was discharged June 27th, 1863.

He married Mary Jane, daughter of Alfred R. Taylor and Larony Sinclair, January 13th, 1864; she died February 12th, 1867, aged twenty-one years and four months. He married for his second wife, Anna M., daughter of Charles Ecklin, December 28th, 1872.

He now resides at Harrington, Delaware, and is engaged in the manufacture of spokes.

Fletcher Bray,

A son of ex-sheriff Wilson and Mary Bray, and grandson of General Daniel Bray, was born in Kingwood Township, Hunterdon County, N. J., December 8th, 1820.

He spent his youthful days on his father's farm, and married Lavinna L., daughter of John L. Larason and Sarah Dean, September 5th, 1849.

He enrolled in Company H, Thirty-Eighth Regiment, New Jersey Volunteers, and was discharged at the end of his enlistment.

He died in Frenchtown, April 26th, 1877. His wife was born December 7th, 1825, and died in Frenchtown, April 1st, 1895. His two sons reside in Philadelphia.

Alonzo Butler,

Son of William Butler and Mahalah Bellis, was born in Alexandria Township, Hunterdon County, New Jersey, March 5th, 1841. He was married to Ann, daughter of Andrew Fleming, of Somerset County, N. J., October 23d, 1869.

He was enrolled in Company D, Eighth Regiment, New Jersey Volunteers, August 29th, 1861, and participated in all the skirmishes

REV. S. D. DECKER.

(See Page 180.)

and battles in which that regiment was engaged, and was discharged September 22d, 1864.

He has followed the occupation of farming since his discharge, and is a prosperous husbandman. He now resides on the road leading from Frenchtown to Everittstown.

Morris Maxwell

Was born in Frenchtown, July 30th, 1824. He was a son of David Maxwell and Lucy Housel. Shortly after his birth his parents moved to Philadelphia, and, his father engaging in the metal working business, he served his apprenticeship with him.

In 1841, he went to sea, and after sailing for seven years to the various parts of the globe, returned to the United States and enlisted in the naval service to do duty on the U. S. Frigate, "Constitution," familiarly known as "Ironsides," and was promoted for meritorious conduct from an ordinary seaman to the position of under keeper.

In 1851, the vessel returned to the United States, and obtaining leave of absence for six weeks, he came to Frenchtown on a visit. While here he resolved to change his manner of living, and having secured a position as tinsmith, he resigned his position in the naval service. He resided in Frenchtown the remainder of his life, following his trade as tinsmith.

He married Delilah A., daughter of William Snyder and Hannah Horner, May 5th, 1853; she died May 6th, 1864, aged thirty-three years, two months and two days.

He married for his second wife, Sarah R., youngest daughter of ex-Judge Isaac R. Srope and Sarah Roelofson, May 29th, 1866.

Mr. Maxwell died in Frenchtown, December 27th, 1892, and his widow, Sarah R., two sons and one daughter survive him.

Mr. Maxwell was a member of the United States Christian Commission, at Washington, D. C., in 1862, and was assigned to duty in the field hospital, and performed his duty faithfully and well.

He was elected collector of Frenchtown in 1884; was a candidate for Mayor in 1881. He was a member of the Common Council in 1871-'74-'77-'78, and when a licence petition was presented to the Common Council to sell liquor, he among others addressed that body in opposition to granting it. It might be truthfully said of him as it was of and by Henry Clay, he would rather be right, than President.

Samuel Hoff,[*]

Son of Thomas Hoff and Ann, daughter of James Dalrymple, was born in Alexandria Township, Hunterdon County, N. J., August 11th, 1843.

He was enrolled in Company G, Fifteenth Regiment, New Jersey Volunteers, August 14th, 1862, and was discharged, June 27th, 1865.

He first married Sarah C., daughter of Emley Hyde and Thisby Dalrymple, September 22d, 1866; she died, January 27th, 1870.

He married for his second wife, Sarah C., daughter of James C. Martin, of Little York, December 13th, 1871.

When he enlisted in the army, he was learning the blacksmith trade, and since his discharge from service has followed the same occupation at Everittstown.

Jacob F. Thatcher

Was a son of Jonas Thatcher, who at one time was a merchant in Frenchtown.

He was enrolled in Company G, Fifteenth Regiment, New Jersey Volunteers, August 14th, 1862, and died in the service of his country from wounds received in the battle of the Wilderness, aged 22 years. His remains are interred at Arlington, Virginia.

Jacob J. Lair

Was a son of Philip D. Lair and Mary Snyder. He was one of a family of five brothers and seven sisters. He learned the trade of tinsmith in Frenchtown, being employed by Gabriel H. Slater and Samuel B. Hudnit. He enlisted in Company G, Fifteenth Regiment, New Jersey Volunteers, July 28th, 1862, and was wounded in the service.

After the close of the war, locating at Lambertville, he married Victoria, daughter of Cornelius Arnett, September 2d, 1868, who is now deceased. He served as a member of Common Council in Lambertville, and was engaged in the store and tinsmith business at the time of his decease, March 4th, 1885. His age was 48 years.

In 1863, from Brandy Station, Virginia, Mr. Lair wrote to the pastor of the Frenchtown M. E. Church, asking if he could be of assistance in

[*]Mr. Hoff is a member of the Everittstown Church. We have taken the liberty to use his name, from the fact, that he with J. J. Lair, made this church a liberal offering while in the army.

REV. MORRIS F. GIBBS.

(See Page 105.)

collecting funds for the advancement of the church ; and receiving an affirmative reply, he collected from the members of Company G, Fifteenth Regiment about seventy-five dollars, and forwarded it to the pastor.

Arthur W. Lundy

Was born in what is now Franklin Township, Hunterdon County, New Jersey, February 6th, 1816.

When a young man, he taught for a number of years in the public schools, but finally learned the trade of watchmaker. When the gold fever broke out in California, in 1848, he with many others from this county went to that State in search of gold. Shortly after returning home he married Theodosia S., daughter of John Reading, of Delaware Township. He has two sons and one daughter.

Mr. Lundy came to Frenchtown in 1851, and has since resided here, following his trade. He did not enter the service of his country, but was a strong advocate of the Union cause. During the war the writer frequently saw him when the newspapers arrived in the morning mails, standing upon an elevation, often on the front porch of the harness shop of Samuel B. Hudnit, reading aloud to the people war news ; he might, in fact have been called the public reader.

In 1861, a meeting was held in the Presbyterian Church in Frenchtown, which was attended by the citizens of the place and vicinity, without distinction of party, sect, or creed, and over thirteen hundred dollars were subscribed for the benefit of the families of those who might enlist in the army, and Henry Lott, Newberry D. Williams, Charles A. Slack, Authur W. Lundy and Samuel B. Hudit, were appointed a committee to distribute the same.

In 1865, when the evacuation of Richmond and its occupancy by our army became known, the church bells of the town were rung for thirty minutes, and a large audience assembled at the station, where patriotic speeches were made by a number of citizens, among whom was Authur W. Lundy. Although now one of our most aged citizens, he enjoys good health and has the esteem and respect of the community.

Gershom L. Everitt,

Son of Benjamin Everitt and Rebecca Rockafellow, was born in the Township of Delaware, Hunterdon County, N. J., December 24th, 1840.

He enlisted in Company F, Thirty-Eighth Regiment, New Jersey Volunteers, September 3d, 1862, and was mustered out June 24th, 1863.

He is now engaged in the flour and feed business, and resides in Frenchtown.

9

Eli Swallow,

A son of Abner Swallow and Amy Salter, was born in Frenchtown, February 12th, 1836. He married Sarah A., daughter of William Reading and Mahalah Rittenhouse, May 10th, 1862. She died suddenly at Riegelsville, Bucks County, Pa., March 5th, 1895.

He enlisted in Company B, Thirty-Eighth Regiment, New Jersey Volunteers, September 5th, 1864, and was discharged June 30th, 1865.

He is a wheelwright by trade, following that occupation in Milford from 1852 to 1856. He located at Frenchtown, May 28th, 1869, and entered into partnership with Jeremiah W. Opdycke in the furniture and undertaking business in 1881. He now resides at Riegelsville, Pa., where he is engaged in the same business as above mentioned.

Mr. Swallow was a member of the Common Council of Frenchtown for six years, and his votes are found recorded in the negative on the question pertaining to the granting of license to sell liquor. He was at one time a freeholder for Frenchtown, and made an excellent record.

Balcer T. Rockafellow,

Son of Isaac and Catharine Rockafellow, enlisted in Company G, Fifteenth Regiment, New Jersey Volunteers, July 28th, 1862, and was discharged December 11th, 1863.

He married Mary Elizabeth, daughter of Peter S. and Mary Martha Taylor. Mr. Taylor died in the service of his country, November 24th, 1862, aged thirty-four years, ten months and twenty days, and is buried in Frenchtown cemetery.

Lorenzo S. D. Kerr,

A son of Abel Kerr and Mary Ann Search, was born near Idell, Kingwood Township, February 21st, 1842, and followed the occupation of farming until he enlisted in Company H, Thirty-Fourth Regiment, New Jersey Volunteers, August 30th, 1864.

He was mustered out of service May 27th, 1865.

He married Mary Ellen, daughter of Richard Wilson and Mary Gaddis, of Raven Rock, Delaware Township, Hunterdon County, N. J., August 30th, 1865, and she died in Frenchtown, May 3d, 1887. He married for his second wife, Martha J., daughter of Emley H. Bellis, and widow of Runyan A. Apgar, May 3d, 1893.

Since the war he has been engaged as farmer, peach grower, lumber dealer, merchant and spoke, hub, sash and blind manufacturer. He is at present a member of the Common Council; he was also a member of this body in 1882-'83. He has four sons and one daughter.

REV. WILLIAM McCAIN.

(See Page 103.)

Edwin Beidelman,

Was born in Nockamixon Township, Bucks County, Pa., June 30th, 1831, and married Mary, daughter of Solomon Trauger.

He enlisted in Company I, Thirty-Eighth Regiment, New Jersey Volunteers, September 4th, 1864, and was discharged June 30th, 1865.

He was a farmer, miller, sawyer and spoke-turner respectively. He served three years as constable in Frenchtown, and died July 9th, 1883.

He has two sons and four daughters living.

Samuel C. Meyers,

A son of Samuel Meyers and Martha Cooper, was born in Tinicum Township, Bucks County, Pa., November 8th, 1834.

He enlisted in Company G, Fifteenth Regiment, August 18th, 1862, and was discharged June 22d, 1865. He participated in the several battles in which his regiment was engaged. Previous to his enlistment he was a sawyer; but since his return from the army he has been engaged in dealing in timber. He resides in Frenchtown.

William H. Stahler,

A son of Daniel Stahler and Mary Ann Snyder, was born in Northampton County, Pa., September 10th, 1840, and came to Frenchtown with his parents in 1852.

He enlisted in Company M, Colonel Corman's Mounted Rifle Rangers, afterwards known as the Eighth Pennsylvania Cavalry, September 24th, 1861, and was discharged September 24th, 1864.

He married Hannah L. Hull, October 12th, 1864, and they have one son. Mr. Stahler served as town clerk of the Borough of Frenchtown for three years. He is now superintendent of the Frenchtown cemetery.

Theodore Sinclair.

Was born in Nockamixon Township, Bucks County, Pa., June 5th, 1829. He enlisted in Company A, Sixteenth New York Infantry, July 1st, 1864, and was discharged for disability, July 16th, 1865. He participated in the battle of Atlanta and Murfreesboro, Ga. He is a mason by trade.

He married, February 5th, 1852, Sarah Ann, daughter of Samuel and Ruth Ecklin, of Kingwood Township, Hunterdon County, N. J. He has three sons, two of whom are living, and one daughter.

Obadiah Stout,

Was a son of Samuel Stout and Sarah, daughter of Obadiah Curtis, was born near the St. Thomas Church, Alexandria Township, Hunterdon County, N. J., November 20th, 1823. He married Amy, daughter of Jacob Fisher and Charity Snyder, December 4th, 1847, and died in Frenchtown, September 11th, 1895.

He was a carpenter by trade, and erected many buildings in Frenchtown.

He enlisted September 4th, 1864, in Company I, Thirty-Eighth Regiment, New Jersey Volunteers, and was discharged at City Point, Virginia, June 30th, 1865.

He held the office of Assessor of Frenchtown for three years. His wife, two sons and two daughters survive him.

Aaron H. Slack,

Was born in Delaware Township, Hunterdon County, N. J., September 24th, 1826. His parents were Henry Slack and Mary Hoagland.

He enlisted in Company E, Third Regiment, New Jersey Volunteers, April 25th, 1861, for three months, and was discharged July 31st, 1861. He reenlisted in Company M, Third New Jersey Cavalry, December 21st, 1863, and was discharged August 1st, 1865.

He crossed the Rapidan with Grant, May 5th, 1864, and was in the battle of the Wilderness. He participated in some of the battles in the Shenandoah Valley, and was wounded in the fight at Summit Station, Virginia.

Mr. Slack is a carpenter by trade, and resides in Frenchtown. He has one son.

Robert B. Lyons,

A native of Bucks County, Pa., resided several years in Frenchtown. He married Lucretia A. Brooks for his first wife, Rachel K. Ashton for his second wife, and Sallie, daughter of Mahlon H. Huffman, for his third wife. He now resides in New Hope, Bucks County, Pa.

He has been engaged in various occupations, such as florist, sash, blind and door manufacturer, carpenter and organ manufacturer. He has three sons and one daughter.

He enlisted in a Company of Bucks County, Pa., and served the term of his enlistment.

REV. E. H. CONKLIN.

(See Page 101.)

Joseph R. Burgstresser,

Was born in Tinicum Township, Bucks County, Pa., February 16th, 1832. He married Fayette, daughter of Joseph Kramer and Catharine Misson, October 20th, 1855.

He enlisted in Company B, Thirty-Eighth Regiment, New Jersey Volunteers, September 3d, 1864, and was discharged at City Point, Virginia, June 30th, 1865. Mr. Burgstresser is a carpenter by trade, and has followed this business since his return from the army. He has four sons and four daughters living.

John V. Gordon,

Son of William Gordon and Henrietta Volk, was born January 21st, 1843, and married Mary C., daughter of George Stull, August 26th, 1863.

He enlisted as a drummer, July 28th, 1862, in Company G, Fifteenth Regiment, New Jersey Volunteers. He was transferred to the Veteran Reserve Corps, March 15th, 1864, and was wounded. He is a brother of Revs. Lewis J. and Janeway Gordon.

After his discharge from the service he was engaged for a time in the grocery business in Frenchtown, but is now a manufacturer of spokes, and resides at Greensburg, Indiana.

Eli Frasier,

Is one of the oldest members of the church that entered the army. He was enrolled in Company F, Thirty-Eighth Regiment, New Jersey Volunteers, September 12th, 1864, and discharged at City Point, Virginia, June 30th, 1865.

He married Caroline, only daughter of George Ecklin, of Kingwood Township, May 24th, 1849. He is a blacksmith by trade, and carried on that work at Frenchtown before his enlistment, and for a time after his return from the army.

He met with an accident January 15th, 1866, which has since prevented him from laboring to any great extent.

Charles F. Nixon,

Was born at Quakertown, Franklin Township, Hunterdon County, N. J., May 2d, 1844. He is a son of Hiram Nixon and Elizabeth H. Opdycke.

He enlisted in Company G, Thirty-Eighth Regiment, New Jersey

Volunteers, September 19th, 1864, and was discharged June 30th, 1865. He married Mamie B., Daughter of Jonathan Eick, April 25th, 1867, and resides in Frenchtown.

George W. Opdycke,

A son of Samuel Opdycke and Christiana, daughter of Hall Opdycke, was born in Alexandria Township, Hunterdon County, N. J., April 19th, 1842. He married Mary E., daughter of John Sine, July 18th, 1868.

He enlisted in Company B, Second New Jersey Cavalry, September 6th, 1864, and was discharged at Vicksburg, Miss., June 29th, 1865. He was wounded in the battle of Egypt Station. He has two sons living.

REV. DAVID CURTIS

(See Page 108.)

CHAPTER VIII.

EPWORTH LEAGUE.

We live to make our church a power in the land, while we live to love every other church that exalts our Christ.—BISHOP SIMPSON.

COMPILED FROM MANUSCRIPTS FURNISHED BY FRANK MAXWELL, MISS KATE TAYLOR AND OTHERS.

ON Tuesday evening, September 30th, 1890, a meeting was held in the M. E. Church for the purpose of organizing an Epworth League. The Pastor, Rev. M. T. Gibbs and Rev. L. J. Gordon, addressed the meeting, setting forth the origin of the Epworth League, its object, and the benefits to be derived from it in a social way, in spreading Christianity among the young people of the town, and in the upbuilding and prosperity of the church. Considerable doubt existed in the minds of many present as to the ultimate success of such an organization, and as a result there was some hesitation evinced in taking hold and proceeding with it. But it was finally agreed to organize, and the following officers were elected to serve for one year:

Pres't., Rev. L. J. Gordon; 1st Vice Pres't., Frank Maxwell; 2d Vice Pres't., Geo. W. Hummer; 3d Vice Pres't., Lizzie Mechling; 4th Vice Pres't., Mrs. G. W. Hummer; Secretary, Miss Kate Taylor; Treasurer, Miss Emma Stout; Organist, Madge Shields.

Twenty-three members were enrolled at this meeting, but this number was increased to thirty-two before the charter was procured, consequently there were thirty-two charter members. The following are the names in the order in which they were enrolled:

Rev. M. T. Gibbs,	Emma Stout,
Mrs. M. T. Gibbs,	Anna Gordon,
Rev. L. J. Gordon,	Frank Maxwell,
Geo. W. Hummer,	Charles Maxwell,
Mrs. Geo. W. Hummer,	John Kline,
Rev. D. M. Matthews,	Geo. E. Slack,
E. W. Bloom,	Peter Stryker,
Mrs. E. W. Bloom,	Mary Hummer,
Kate Taylor,	Fred Bloom,

Madge Shields,   Mrs. Fred Bloom,
Lavinia Shields,   Mrs. Wm. R. Shurtz,
Lizzie Burgstresser,   Mrs. Wilbur Slack,
Anna Wells,   Wm. W. Housel,
Watson Blakeslee,   Lina Mechling,
Lizzie Maxwell,   Cora Lair,
Lizzie Mechling,   Lizzie Hinkle.

The first Epworth League devotional meeting was held in the church the Sunday evening following its organization, and these meetings have been kept up with great interest ever since.

The first business meeting at which the Constitution and By-Laws of the League were adopted, was held October 20th, 1890, and the first meeting of the Cabinet, October 30th, 1890. It was decided to hold the annual business meeting for the election of officers, the second Wednesday evening in October, and the monthly business meeting the second Wednesday evening in each month. An Epworth training class was organized to prepare the youthful workers for the Master's service. A Watchnight service was held on New Year's Eve, at which time the Everittstown League was present and participated in the exercises. At this meeting the greatest revival in the history of the church was begun, it continued for about two months and during its progress over one hundred persons professed conversion. The membership of the League increased during the year to 144. There were held during the year fifty-three devotional meetings, fourteen business meetings, two socials and three entertainments.

Chapter 3,912 of the Epworth League accomplished much during its first year; much more than its most sanguine friends could have anticipated.

SECOND YEAR.

Though the anniversary of its birth was not publicly observed, the League was no less fruitful in good works, and the following officers were elected for the year:

Pres't., Rev. L. J. Gordon; 1st Vice Pres't., Mrs. M. T. Gibbs; 2d Vice Pres't., F. B. Fargo; 3d Vice Pres't., Lizzie Mechling; 4th Vice Pres't., Mrs. Geo. W. Hummer; Secretary, Miss Kate Taylor; Treasurer, Emma Stout; Organist, —— ——.

The League held during the year fifty devotional meetings, fourteen business meetings and ten literary meetings, eighteen persons joined during the year. Total number enrolled, 162. Several members removed from town and joined other Leagues. Two have died—Anna

REV. LEWIS J. GORDON.

(See Page 105.)

B. Opdyke and Madge R. Shields. The League held special Thanksgiving and Christmas services, and also an Anniversary service was held Sabbath, May 15th, the day was ushered in by a sunrise prayer meeting which was well attended, forty-five subscribers were obtained for the *Epworth Herald*. The department of literary work organized a reading circle, December 14th, with Miss Kate Taylor as Chairman, and Anna Wells as Secretary, a course of reading was pursued, which was quite successful for a time, but for lack of interest it was finally abandoned.

THIRD YEAR.

The following officers were elected :

Pres't., G. W. Hummer; 1st Vice Pres't., J. C. Butler; 2d Vice Pres't., Mrs. Wm. R. Shurtz; 3d Vice Pres't, Charles Maxwell; 4th Vice Pres't., Leina Mechling; Secretary, Kate Taylor; Treasurer, Lizzie Maxwell; Organist, Stella Hoffman.

Fifty-two devotional meetings were held during the year, fourteen business and three cabinet meetings, special Thanksgiving, Watchnight and Anniversary services were held. Two delegates attended the State convention at Newark. 100 copies of Epworth Songs were purchased; twenty-eight subscribers obtained for the *Epworth Herald*. Nine persons joined the League during the year, and a Junior Epworth League with forty members was organized.

FOURTH YEAR.

The time for the annual election of officers was changed this year from October to January, to be in uniformity with the other Leagues of the State. Also changed the monthly business meeting to the second Friday evening of each month. The following officers were elected :

Pres't., G. W. Hummer; 1st Vice Pres't., J. C. Butler; 2d Vice Pres't., Mrs. N. J. Tomer; 3d Vice Pres't, Rev. D. M. Matthews; 4th Vice Pres't., Mrs. D. M. Everitt; Secretary, Kate Taylor; Treasurer, Lizzie Maxwell; Organist, Lizzie Maxwell.

Sixty-four devotional and thirteen business meetings, and one cabinet meeting held during the year. Anniversary exercises were held Sabbath, May 14th. Thanksgiving and Watchnight were observed with appropriate services, five dollars were sent to the Treasurer in response to an appeal for Missions. Twenty-five subscribers were obtained for the *Herald*, and seventy copies of the revival number were distributed among the members. Three delegates and a number of Leaguers attended the State Convention at Camden, May 9th, 10th.

Sixty members of the League attended the first rally of the Epworth County Union, at Quakertown, August 18th, the second rally was held at Frenchtown, December, 12th. This meeting was largely attended, though the weather was bad, and was both instructive and inspiring. During the months of July and August the department of spiritual work took charge of the Sabbath evening services.

FIFTH YEAR.

On January 11th, 1895, the annual business meeting of the League was held, at which time the following officers were elected:

Pres't., Frank Maxwell; 1st Vice Pres't., Rev. L. J. Gordon; 2d Vice Pres't., Mrs. N. J. Tomer; 3d Vice Pres't., W. D. Nichols; 4th Vice Pres't., Mrs. D M. Everitt; Secretary, Lizzie Maxwell; Treasurer, Clarence Fargo; Organist, Mrs. Belle Webster.

During the year an Epworth League Chorus was organized, which greatly adds to the interest of the devotional meetings.

SIXTH YEAR.

The time for the annual election of officers was again changed to October, the following list is the result of the election for this year:

Pres't., Frank Maxwell; 1st Vice Pres't., G. W. Hummer; 2d Vice Pres't., Mrs. T. W. Holcombe; 3d Vice Pres't., J. Butler; 4th Vice Pres't., W. D. Nichols; Secretary, Lizzie Maxwell; Treasurer, Cora Hoff; Organist, Mrs. Belle Webster.

The following is a list of the members at the present time, January, 1896.

Rev. L. J. Gordon,	Laura Woolverton,
Geo. W. Hummer,	Lorenzo D. Reigle,
Mrs. Geo. W. Hummer,	Theo. W. Holcombe,
Rev. D. M. Matthews,	Mrs. Theo. W. Holcombe,
E. W. Bloom,	Stella Hoffman,
Mrs. E. W. Bloom,	Frank F. Maxwell,
Kate Taylor,	Mrs. Ernest Stryker,
Lizzie R. Maxwell,	John Hoffman,
John H. Kline,	Anna Misson,
Mrs. John H. Kline,	Bertha Slack,
Emma Stout,	Laura Keeler,
Charles S. Maxwell,	Josie Plum,
Peter Stryker,	Nellie Warford,
Mary Hummer,	Cora Hoff,
Ernest Stryker,	Jennie J. Rittenhouse,
Mrs. Wm. R. Shurtz,	Mrs. Orville Cole,

FRANK F. MAXWELL.
President of Epworth League.

Carrie Roberson,
Mrs. Jacob Bunn,
Anna Belle Niece,
Nathan L. Shurtz,
Wilbur S. Holcombe,
Mrs. Wm. Silverthorn,
Emma Johnson,
Anna R. Wright,
Chas. Philkill,
Thos. M. Pinkerton,
Harry S. Slack,
Mrs. H. C. Roberson,
Josiah Butler,
Mrs. J. Butler,
Mrs. Sam'l Snyder,
Mrs. Henry Cronce,
Chas. K. Hummer,
Wm. H. Sipes,
Mrs. Hugh Taylor,
I. L. Niece,
Mrs. I. L. Niece,
Wm. E. Culver,
Harvey Gruver,
Mrs. Harvey Gruver,
Sylvester B. Horner,
Mrs. Sylvester Horner,
Sam'l R. Dalrymple,
F. B. Fargo,
Mrs. Sam'l Dalrymple,
Mrs. L. J. Gordon,
Mrs. John Lantz,
D. W. C. Case,
Lucy B. Case,
Mrs. F. B. Fargo,
Laura Bonham,
Chas. B. Salter,
Mrs. Chas. B. Salter,
Lavinia Case,
William Hawk,
Lila Nixon,
John Kugler, Jr.,
Clarence B. Fargo,
Mrs. D. W. C. Case,

Edgar J. Hawk,
Mrs. Edgar J. Hawk,
Frank Roberson,
Mrs. D. M. Everitt,
Emma C. Hoff,
Geo. F. Bloom,
Mrs. Geo. F. Bloom,
Frank Niece,
Mrs. John McClain,
Linnie Srope,
Florence McClain,
N. J. Tomer,
Mrs. N. J. Tomer,
Alfred Curtis,
Elmer E. Culver,
Arthur G. Able,
Charles B. Tomer,
Nellie Buckley,
Sylvester Reigle,
Mrs. Sylvester Reigle,
Lucy Johnson,
Nellie Rittenhouse,
Mrs. Richard Lanning,
Austin Stout,
C. H. Swick,
Mrs. C. H. Swick,
Mrs. Chas. R. Everitt,
Mrs. Aaron H. Slack,
Mrs. Wilbur Slack,
Will D. Nichols,
Samuel Bloom,
Andrew K. Kinney,
Mrs. Andrew Kinney,
Wm. C. Kline,
Mrs. Belle M. Webster,
Charlie Stamets,
Fred Bloom,
Mrs. Fred Bloom,
Rev. E. H. Conklin,
Mrs. E. H. Conklin,
Ida May Conklin,
Wm. J. Conklin,
Mrs. Wm. O. Roberson.

JUNIOR EPWORTH LEAGUE.

BY CLARENCE B. FARGO.

The Junior Epworth League was organized in 1893, by Rev. Wm. McCain, with the following officers:

Sup't., Miss Laura Woolverton; Secretary, Nellie Swick; Treasurer, Clarence Fargo.

It did not become a chartered League until March 17th, 1894, when it was listed as number 2,402.

Formerly the devotional services of the League were held on Thursday afternoons, after the sessions of the public schools, but was subsequently changed to Sunday afternoon, after the Sabbath School session, as more members would be likely to attend.

Various means have been used to hold the interest of the children in this work.

A book entitled "Daily Food" was offered to each member who recited the ten commandments, and they were also appointed to lead the devotional services.

The present officers are as follows:

Sup't, Mrs. Chas. Salter; Ass't. Sup't., Mrs. R. Lanning; Pres't., Austin Stout; Vice Pres't., Charles Tomer; Secretary, Allie Lanning; Treasurer, Lida Hoff.

The League numbers seventy-eight members as follows:

Jessie Hummer,	Willie Bloom,
Lida Hoff,	John Phile,
May Misson,	Sammie Culver,
Annie Tomer,	Cleve Culver,
Bertha Curtis,	Frank Poulson,
Rowenna Fargo,	Herman Smith,
Lottie Salter,	Roy Hewitt,
Tillie Culver,	Carol Gruver,
Mabel Hoff,	Gussie Lippencott,
Charles B. Tomer,	Harry Sinclair,
Lewis Hoff,	Sammie Sinclair,
Snyder Hoff,	Peter Sinclair,
Clarence B. Fargo,	Fred M. Gordon,
Frank Fargo,	Russel Bloom,
Austin Stout,	Chester Niece,
Chester Lancaster,	Horace Everitt,
Charles Lancaster,	Frank Everitt,

Lottie Sinclair,
Bertie Bancroft,
Lizzie Schaible,
Albert Lanning,
Eugene Lanning,
Fred Schaible,
Lydia Edwards,
Fred Robinson,
Emily Apgar,
Wilda McClain,
Richie Kerr,
Walter Robinson,
Emily Opdyke,
Dale Opdyke,
Cynthia Britton,
Belle Britton,
Belle Stahler,
Clifford Hawk,
Dory Pinkerton,
Frank Pinkerton,
Ella Hyde,
Ida May Salter,

Nellie Lantz,
Bertha Burket,
Carrie Stryker,
Lizzie Snyder,
Willie Hill,
Bertha Bloom,
Earl Rittenhouse,
Russel Lantz,
Raymond Loper,
Sadie Snyder,
Georgie Snyder,
Frank McClain,
Eliza Major,
Emma Edwards,
Linnie Srope,
Mary Misson,
Ella Niece,
Lena Everitt,
Charles Stamets,
Raymond Slack,
Willie Bloom,
Florence Srope.

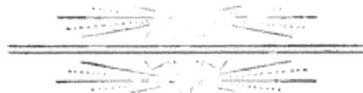

CHAPTER IX.

A Brief History of the Sunday School, with a List of Superintendents; a List of the Trustees of the Church from
1845 to 1895; Ladies' Aid Society with a List of Members.

A Brief History of the Sunday School,

BY

George W. Hummer.

"The Sunday School, the Sunday School.
It is the place I love ;
For there I learn the Golden Rule
That leads to joys above."

IN PRESENTING this brief history of the Sunday School, together
with a list of superintendents as complete as circumstances have
made it possible to secure, it must be remembered that no data has
been found by which light can be thrown upon the many important
and interesting incidents connected with its early growth, or upon its
methods of procedure; but, with the material at hand, we shall
endeavor to present it as best we can to the reader.

The Sunday School was organized in the summer of 1845, during the
ministration of Rev. A. M. Palmer, in the gallery on the east side of
the church, there being no basement at that time, with David Moore
as superintendent.

The sessions of the school were held regularly every Sabbath morning
in the gallery ; and, as the school was connected with the schools of
Quakertown and Everittstown and thus united a long time, there are
no available means by which we can ascertain what the strength of
membership was, neither are there any authentic records in our possession to even name the teachers.

Mrs. Amy Pittenger informs us that she was appointed the first
primary teacher in 1863, and in one month she succeeded in establishing a class of over thirty children. In 1864, for the first time, we find
that the school was reported to the quarterly conference as being in a
prosperous condition, with ninety scholars and eighteen teachers.

On December 11th, 1870, in an address made by superintendent

BOARD OF STEWARDS.

BENJ. PHILKILL, E. W. BLOOM, ANDREW K. KINNEY, D. W. C. CASE, ED. RITTENHOUSE,

G. W. HUMMER,   I. L. NIECE,   H. B. HAWK,   JOHN H. KLINE.

Obadiah Stout, we find the statement that "twenty-one years ago the school numbered three teachers and twenty-five scholars," and this statement, coming from one who knew whereof he spoke, throws light upon the strength of the school in the closing days of '49.

In 1870, the membership of the school was 178, average attendance 125, with a total collection of $28.09.

To illustrate the steady increase in membership and financial support since 1881, from which time we have complete records, we can authoritively state that at the close of 1881, the school numbered six officers, fifteen teachers and 115 scholars; average attendance seventy-three, and collection amounting to $21.10; and at the close of 1894, the records show a membership of 200, average attendance 134, amount of collection, $134. 51 besides $48.94 for missionary purposes.

Thus hath God blessed and propered our school! Thus hath His smile been upon it through all the years of its existence! And our sincere hope and prayer is that it may be so guided and directed in the future as to continue to merit that smile of approval and that blessing of prosperity! May it be the means of so imprinting the love of God on the hearts of the young, that they may be brought to a saving knowledge of sins forgiven; that they, their superintendent and teachers, may all meet in that beautiful home above and dwell forever with the Lord!

In the gracious revival of '91, fifty-one members of the Sunday school united with the church, showing what a powerful factor the Sunday school is to the advancement of Christianity, and how much every Sunday school worker should be encouraged to labor on, and meet and overcome every obstacle that may arise.

> " For we know not when we scatter,
>   Where the precious seed will fall ;
>   But we work and trust in Jesus,
>   For He watcheth over all."

The following is a list of Superintendents :

David Moore, 1845–'52.

Joseph Ashton, 1853–'54.

Peter Risler, 1855–'56.

Morris Maxwell, 1857–'59 ; 1861–'65 ; 1868–'69 ; 1879–'81.

David S. Burwell, 1860.

Andrew Slack, 1866.

Obadiah Stout, 1867, 1870 to 1875.

W. H. Stahler, 1876.

J. E. Cook, 1877–'78.

G. W. Hummer, 1881–'95.

The following is a list of the Trustees from 1844 to 1895, as far as we have been able to ascertain:

WRITTEN BY JOHN L. SLACK, Esq.

Lewis M. Prevost, 1844-'47.

Cyrenius A. Slack, 1844-'47, 1855-'57.

Ambrose Silverthorn, 1844-'50.

John V. Hull, 1844-'48.

Sylvester R. Chamberlain, 1844.

John Rodenbaugh, 1844.

Charles Shuster, 1844-'46.

Thomas Roberson, 1845.

William Roberson, 1845.

Samuel L. Hoff, 1846-'47.

Samuel Pittenger, 1846-'48.

Solomon Stout, 1848-'50.

David Moore, 1850-'53.

Richard Stockton, 1850-'53.

Ralph Ten Eyck, 1850-'51.

Obadiah Stout, 1850-'58, 1860-'67, 1870-'72, 1880-'81, 1886-'88.

Charles Green, 1851-'54.

Joseph Ashton, 1851-'65.

Eli Frazier, 1851-'53.

Samuel B. Hudnit, 1852-'56, 1860 '64.

Ozias P. Thatcher, 1852-'56.

George Rounsaval, 1854-'56.

Morris Maxwell, 1854-'57, 1860-'62, 1866, 1869-'77, 1889-'91.

Levi Case, 1857, 1860-'64.

Samuel Rockafellow, 1860-'64, 1868-'72, 1881.

Silas S. Wright, 1861-'62.

Andrew Slack, 1866-'68, 1873-'74, 1877-'79.

Adam S. Haring, 1867-'80.

Peter Y. Lowe, 1867-'69.

David Roberson, 1867-'72, 1879-'80.

Francis B. Fargo, 1877, 1879-'80, 1889-'95.

Joseph Aller, 1868, 1881-'84.

Reeder T. Slack, 1868.

Morris L. Morgan, 1868.

Edward Lair, 1869, 1883.

George H. Sanders, 1869-'70.

R. K. Niece, 1869-'72.

John L. Slack, 1870-'81, 1884-'92, 1895.

David Curtis, 1870-'72, 1881-'87.

Munson Baldwin, 1871-'76, 1881-'82.

Joseph E. Cook, 1873-'78.

Benjamin Phillkill, 1873-'75, 1885-'89.

Edwin Beidelman, 1875-'83.

D. M. Matthews, 1876-'85.

Thomas R. Opdyke, 1877.

Levi M. Hice, 1878.

Eli Swallow, 1878, 1881-'88.

Janeway Gordon, 1879.

H. W. Bellis, 1882.

G. W. Hummer, 1882, 1890-'95.

T. W. Holcombe, 1883-'85.

Edward Rittenhouse, 1883.

L. S. D. Kerr, 1883-'85, 1891-'95.

Hiram Danly, 1886.

Peter C. Mechling, 1886-'91.

Levi M. Hoffman, 1887-'94.

George Stintsman, 1888.

E. W. Bloom, 1889-'95.

John H. Kline, 1890.

William V. Gordon, 1890.

Josiah Butler, 1891-'95.

William Niece, 1891-'95.

I. L. Niece, 1892-'95.

Alfred Curtis, 1893-'95.

LADIES' AID SOCIETY OF FRENCHTOWN M. E. CHURCH.

Mrs E. W. Bloom.

The present Ladies' Aid Society of the Frenchtown M. E. Church, was organized May 15th, 1890, by Rev. M. T. Gibbs, with seven charter members.

The officers were as follows:

Pres't., Mrs. M. T. Gibbs; Vice Pres't., Mrs. Geo. W. Hummer; Secretary, Mrs. E. W. Bloom; Treasurer, Mrs. T. W. Holcombe.

The Society holds its meetings the third Wednesday evening in each month; the money paid in for dues, and what is realized by sociables, entertainments, and various contributions, is used for the benefit of the parsonage, and for other useful objects of the church.

The Society is in a flourishing condition, having at the present time thirty-five members, and has collected since its organization $275.

The officers at the present time are:

Pres't., Mrs. E. W. Bloom; Vice Pres't., Mrs. E. H. Conklin; Secretary, Mrs. John H. Kline: Treasurer, Mrs. J. E. Sherman; Collector, Mrs. Mary Pinkerton.

The following is the present membership:

Mrs. Mary Pinkerton,	Mrs. E. H. Conklin,
Mrs. H. F. Gruver,	Mrs. Wm. O. Roberson,
Mrs. Hugh Eichlin,	Mrs. S. R. Dalrymple,
Mrs. L. D. Hagaman,	Mrs. John L. Roberson,
Mrs. Geo. W. Hummer,	Mrs. D. M. Everitt,
Mrs. Judson Hoff,	Mrs. Susan L. Reading,
Mrs. E. W. Bloom,	Hrs. F. B. Fargo,
Mrs. Sylvester Horner,	Mrs. Chas. B. Salter,
Mrs. Sarah Atkinson,	Mrs. H. I. Srope,
Mrs. John H. Kline,	Mrs. J. E. Sherman,
Mrs. J. Butler,	Mrs. Wm. R. Shurtz,
Mrs. A. S. Lanning,	Mrs. N. J. Tomer,
Mrs. Geo. F. Bloom,	Mrs. Johnson Warford,
Mrs. Wm. Niece,	Mrs. Elizabeth Wright,
Mrs. Chas. P. Bissey,	Mrs. Henry Quirk,
Mrs. I. L. Niece,	Miss Lizzie Stout,
Mrs. Harriet Barcroft,	Miss Emma Stout.
Mrs. Benj. Philkill,	

MEMBERS OF THE LADIES AID SOCIETY.

CHAPTER X.

SEMI-CENTENNIAL EXERCISES; BRIEF OUTLINES OF SERMONS;
SUBSCRIPTION LIST FOR THE SEMI-CENTENNIAL BOOK.

BY REV. E. H. CONKLIN.

THE Semi-Centennial celebration of the Methodist Episcopal Church, of Frenchtown, was suggested by the Rev. D. M. Matthews, at the Second Quarterly Conference held August 28th, 1895. The conference was favorable to the suggestion and appointed a committee of six to have charge of the celebration. The following were the committee: D. M. Matthews, J. L. Slack, Josiah Butler, I. L. Neice, G. W. Hummer, E. H. Conklin.

It was resolved to celebrate during the week commencing with the 15th of December, 1895, and the first service was held on Monday evening, the 16th. The committee authorized the publication of a program which was to contain the order of exercises for the entire week. We had a most auspicious opening, good roads, a clear sky, and the presence of the first speaker on the list, Rev. Thomas E. Gordon, of Harrison, N. J. In beginning his remarks, he said that it was with considerable effort that he resisted the inclination to turn aside from the text and take up the recollections of his pleasant and fruitful pastorate of Frenchtown. One circumstance he must mention. It was the commencement of a revival during his second year. He came to the last of the week with scarcely any preparation for the Sabbath. Not because he had failed to labor, for he had worked hard, but because the accomplishment of what was ordinarily easy, seemed at this particular time impossible. Saturday afternoon came and found him with no sermon for the Sabbath.

It was purely providential that he met on the evening of that day, Mrs. Julia Bryant of Washington, N. J., to whom he related his experience. After finding out that Mrs. Bryant was an Evangelist, he said, " you must preach for me to-morrow morning." Which she finally consented to do. Her text was from the twelfth of Romans, " I beseech you, therefore, brethren, by the mercies of God, that ye present your bodies a living sacrifice" &c., &c. At the conclusion of the sermon, Brother Gordon invited all who would comply with the request of the text, to come forward and kneel at the altar. He closed his eyes, somewhat afraid of the result, but when he opened them he saw the aisles filled with the coming people. And soon all available space about the altar was occupied with kneeling supplicants, and from that moment the work went on without interruption until fifty or sixty persons were converted.

Mr. Gordon took his text from the prophesy of Jeremiah, eighth chapter and twentieth verse, "The harvest is past, the summer is ended, and we are not saved." His subject was our fleeting spiritual privileges. He first spoke of the power of Christ to save, and told a story of Bishop James, who made repeated endeavors to save a physician, who was addicted to the drink habit. He fell away many times, but as often as he fell the Bishop would "look up and lift up" until finally he was permanently restored; a proof of the power of Jesus to save to the utmost. Among the fleeting privileges were the intercessions of Christ, the moving power of the Holy Ghost, and the blessing of choice.

Tuesday, December 17th, was the Anniversary Day. A little after six o'clock the bell struck for fifty years of church history. Rev. I. N. VanSant was the preacher for the evening. The words of his text were "If I be lifted up from the earth, I will draw all men unto me," (John twelve and thirty-two.) He made the statement that Christ was actually drawing all men unto Himself at the present time, and quoted the saying of the Great Napoleon: "My generals leave me, I cannot hold them; but increasing millions follow the standard of Christ."

The drawing power of the cross was compared to a magnet. Sir Isaac Newton carried a very small one in his pocket, it weighed only three grains, but its lifting power was 756 grains. Cards placed between the magnet and the object to be lifted diminished the drawing power, and the more numerous the cards the less the pull of the magnet. It was so with Christians who allowed sinful pleasures, love of money, worldliness, to come between Christ and themselves. Rust is a non-conductor, and where it gathers on iron it is so much hinderance to the magnet; and the accumulations of wickedness, like rust, will interfere with the attractive power of Christ. The magnet not only attracts to itself, but it also magnetizes whatever is brought into contract with, so that a nail being magnetized becomes itself a magnet to draw other nails to itself. So Christians filled with the Christ Spirit, act on others to draw them to the Saviour. Another thought concerning the magnet was that its power was exclusively exerted on inferior metals; it does not act on gold, silver, pearls, precious stones, but iron. Jesus, speaking of the best classes of society, said, "the publicans and harlots go into the kingdom of heaven before you." He came not to call the righteous, but sinners to repentence.

The Rev. William McCain was on the program for Wednesday evening, but was in the midst of extra meetings at the time and could not be present. The Rev. John McMuarray, of Finesville, very kindly consented to preach in his stead. He took his text from the Book of Acts, eleven and twenty-four, " A good man full of the Holy Ghost and of faith." He said that the three qualities spoken of in the text, goodness, faith, and the fullness of the blessing of the Holy Spirit were the essential qualities in Christian character. A man might attain success in some departments of life with little or no morality, but character was absolutely necessary for prosperous service in the Master's vineyard. We might have many other things that would help us toward success, riches, intellect, personal influence, but these are worthless without goodness, faith, and spiritual power.

The Rev. W. E. Blakeslee was with us on Thursday evening, and preached a very earnest, gospel sermon from the text, " A sower went forth to sow." (Matthew, thirteen and three.) He prefaced his sermon by saying that it seemed like visiting his birth-place, to come to Frenchtown. It was thirty years ago last spring since he left this town. The country at that time was passing through the fire and blood of the great civil conflict. Many changes have come since then. He could recognize only a very few who were in the church when he was pastor.

His first thought on the text was, that the sower was a man, and he could not tell why God had selected man to sow the seed of the kingdom, but He had. It was a great honor to be associated with God in labor. Man went among men, and the material on which he labored was imperishable. Men work on clay or marble or granite and produce results for time. But he who scatters the seeds of truth, touches the immortal mind, and his work extends into eternity. The seed is the word of God and when planted must grow. It contains a life principle, and as sure as it is dropped into appropriate soil it will spring up. Sometimes we may grow discouraged because results seem so far away. We are to remember, however, that the command is, not to reap, but to sow. Two returned Missionary workers related the history of their labors. One told how God had blessed his efforts, how churches had been built, what multitudes of souls had been saved. The other hearing such a glowing report, could scarcely be induced to speak. He had toiled through the night of years and had caught nothing. He had seen no such results as his brother Missionary, but this one thing gave him heart; he remembered the words of the Lord

Jesus, how He did not say, "Well done good and *successful* servant, but, well done good and *faithful* servant, enter into the joy of thy Lord." God rewards faithfulness rather than success. The sower went forth, and did not wait for the soil to come to him, but went forth. So are we to go forth, out in the highway, out in the by-way, the office, the shop, the saloon, wherever man can be found, and declare the truth by word and example. The preacher did not only speak to the ministry, but to the rank and file. We are all to go forth. Brother Blakeslee was greeted by a large congregation, and after the benediction was pronounced many of the old friends gathered about the preacher. Some were converted during the last year of his ministry in Frenchtown. They had been faithful, and the greetings were much like they shall be in the heavenly life. Great joy at the discovery of so many saved, with the added happiness that we shall go no more out forever.

Friday evening the pastors of the sister churches of the town were present. The Rev. Charles M. Deitz of the Baptist Church gave a very interesting address on the Jubilee year. It was at this Jewish festival that all debts were cancelled, all slaves were set free, the ground was not tilled, and every man was to return to his former possessions. He called attention to the spiritual significance of these thoughts. We should be joyful, we should exercise the grace of forgiveness and mercy, and work for the deliverance of souls in bondage to sin. The words of the preacher were words of counsel and kindly greeting and were highly appreciated by the people.

The Rev. W. H. Filson of the Presbyterian Church, began by quoting the words of St. Paul as he landed at Appii-forum, and his friends from Rome met him. "Whom, when Paul saw, he thanked God and took courage," (Acts twenty-eight and fifteen.) So this church, as it passes the fiftieth mile stone, has reason to thank God and look with brightest hopes on the future. He then reviewed the events in the development of the nations of the world during this time and especially of this nation. He then spoke on what the church had done in her advance movements as illustrated by Missions, Sabbath schools, Young People's organizations &c. Then he spoke of the blessedness of having had the pure gospel preached in this church during the last half century. Expanding this idea, he spoke of the grandeur of the church and in what it consists.

1. It did not consist in her antiquity.
2. Not in architecture.
3. Not in ritual.
4. Not in the union of church and state.
5. Not in wealth.
6. Not in members.

Each of these is claimed by their respective advocates as constituting the true grandeur of the church. But the Jewish Church possessed all of these and yet God repudiated it.

The true grandeur of the church lies in the work of saving souls and in protecting and developing them.

The elements of her grandeur are :

1. Possession of the truth.
2. Love of the truth.
3. Obedience to the truth.
4. Charity—Paul, " More excellent way."
5. Success in saving souls.
6. Faithfulness in instructing converts.

To reach this, earnest men are needed. May this church never lack in any of the essentials of successful church work, and may her increasing years bring to her perpetual and eternal youth ; strong in the Lord and the power of His might.

On Saturday evening, the Epworth League held a service. The program was as follows :

Service of Song, - - - - - - - *Epworth Chorus.*
Prayer and Scripture Reading, - - - - - - *Pastor.*
Historical Sketch, - - - - - - - *Frank Maxwell.*
The League and the Church, - - - - *Rev. L. J. Gordon.*
Vocal Solo—Fear not Ye, O, Israel, - - *Miss Janet Williams.*
Address - - - - - - - - *Rev. A. M. Palmer.*
Address - - - - - - - - *Rev. Joseph Gaskill.*
Doxology and Benediction.

Sabbath, December 22th, 1895. On this day we were favored with the presence of two men who ministered to the people more than fifty years ago. Rev. A. M. Palmer of Newark Conference, who was pastor when the church was dedicated, and also Rev. Joseph Gaskill, who in 1842, organized a class of eleven members. During the morning service at which Rev. A. M. Palmer preached, the pastor of the church asked if there were any present who were connected with this church fifty years ago; four persons arouse, Mrs. Hannah Slack, Mrs. Catharine Wannamaker, Mrs. Andrew Slack and Mrs. John L. Slack. The question was then asked if there were any present who were connected with the charge fifty years ago, and five more arose, viz : William Large, Esq., of Quakertown, Samuel Dalrymple and Mahlon Rittenhouse, of Everittstown, Mrs. Emma Eckel, of Washington and Mrs. Lavinia Pittenger, of Frenchtown.

A Semi-Centennial offering was taken in aid of the trustees, amounting to one hundred and fifteen dollars.

The Semi-Centennial sermon was preached by Rev. A. M. Palmer. It is omitted from this volume for want of room, but may appear in pamphlet form.

Sabbath school anniversary was held in the afternoon under the direction of Brother G. W. Hummer, superintendent of the school, the exercises consisted of singing, also an historical address by Brother Hummer, and speeches by former superintendents.

Andrew Slack and William Stahler, Miss Emma Moore, the daughter of the first superintendent of the school, also made some remarks.

Rev. Joseph Gaskill preached in the evening to a very large and attentive audience.

The following is a brief sketch of his sermon:

The text was found in the Gospel of John, first chapter and forty-second verse.

John the Baptist was born some forty miles from Jerusalem and about seventy miles from Nazareth, the home of Jesus. He was born about six months before Jesus. It seems from the history that the mothers of these distinguished persons were intimate friends, if not related. In their youth these children were strangers to each other and had probably never met until the meeting on the bank of the Jordon. John commenced his ministry when about thirty years of age in the hill country of Judea and about the Jordan.

He preached with such telling effect that multitudes came to hear and were baptized of him, confessing their sins. Then cometh Jesus from Galilee to the Jordon to be baptized of him. The next day John seeth Jesus coming unto him, saith, "Behold the Lamb of God which taketh away the sin of the world." The next day as he saw Him walk he saith, "Behold the Lamb of God!" Two of His disciples standing near, heard him speak and followed Jesus. Jesus turned and saw them following, and saith "what seek ye?" They say unto Him, "Rabbi where dwellest thou?" He saith, "come and see." They came and saw and abode with Him that day. One of the two disciples was Andrew, Simon Peter's brother; he findeth his own brother Simon, and saith unto him, "we have found the Messias, which is the Christ," and he brought him to Jesus.

The central thought of the text is, influence or the means used to bring men to Jesus.

1. Knowledge of Jesus and the Scriptures.
2. Love of Jesus and His own brother Simon.
3. Faith in Jesus as the Son of God.
4. Gift of the Holy Ghost.
5. The example of a holy life.

Brother Matthews wrote on page 27 in regard to our semi-centennial that "an advance movement is expected in every department of Christian work."

I want to add to the glory of God we have not been disappointed. Up to date, February 11th, 1896, fifty-five persons have professed conversion, the most of whom have united with the church, and the meetings still continue.

SEMI-CENTENNIAL HYMN.

BY J. F. DODD, D. D.

Our fathers' God, to Thee we raise
Our hearts this day in grateful praise ;
For all Thy love and mercy shown,
To those whom here Thou long hast known.

Full fifty years of toil and care,
By honored saints in faith and prayer,
Has brought Thy constant blessing down,
With good success their work to crown.

Thy word hath here been uttered long,
In sermon, speech and joyful song ;
By faithful men, with zeal and love,
With holy unction from above.

Its power, as of old displayed,
Hath many precious converts made ;
Of whom some to this hour remain,
While others with the Saviour reign.

Now, gracious God, let blessings come,
On this old and honored home ;
And as the years flow on apace,
Endow her with abiding grace.

SUBSCRIBERS

Semi-Centennial History of the Frenchtown M. E. Church.

NAME.	ADDRESS.	NAME.	ADDRESS.
Alfred Curtis, Frenchtown.		Fred Bloom, Locktown.	
G. W. Hummer, Frenchtown.		Sophia T. Hough, Frenchtown.	
Josiah Butler, Frenchtown.		K. F. Henarie, Frenchtown.	
Andrew Slack, Frenchtown.		E. Rittenhouse, Frenchtown.	
F. B. Fargo, Frenchtown.		Charles B. Salter, Frenchtown.	
W. Lambert Rice, Mt. Pleasant.		Michael Uhler, Uhlertown, Pa.	
E. W. Bloom, Frenchtown.		H. B. Hawk, Uhlertown, Pa.	
S. M. Rittenhouse, Frenchtown.		David Roberson, Frenchtown.	
Hon. W. H. Martin, Frenchtown.		Will D. Nichols, Frenchtown.	
W. H. Sipes, Frenchtown.		Levi Case, Milford.	
B. Philkill, Frenchtown.		James E. Sherman, Frenchtown.	
W. T. Srope, Esq., Frenchtown.		Augustus Cronce, Frenchtown.	
L. S. D. Kerr, Frenchtown.		Samuel A. Besson, Hoboken.	
Frank F. Maxwell, Frenchtown.		H. W. Cronce, Everittstown.	
Hon. C. N. Reading, Frenchtown.		S. H. Wright, Everittstown.	
Edward Hinkle, Frenchtown.		John W. Lequear, Frenchtown.	
Rev. L. J. Gordon, Frenchtown.		Isaac T. Cronce, Frenchtown.	
Gershom L. Everitt, Frenchtown.		Joseph Ashton, Sr., Trenton.	
Thomas Holland, Everittstown.		Alonzo Butler, Frenchtown.	
John H. Matthews, Mt. Pleasant.		E. W. Opdyke, Frenchtown.	
John H. Kline, Frenchtown.		Sarah K. Walbert, Frenchtown.	
Hezekiah Hoff, Frenchtown.		George Stintsman, Frenchtown.	
J. L. Slack, Esq., Frenchtown.		Wilbur Slack, Frenchtown.	
W. H. Stahler, Frenchtown.		A. S. Haring, Hagerstown, Md.	
W. Large, Esq., Quakertown.		Abel B. Haring, Frenchtown.	
Deborah A. Hill, Frenchtown.		C. Rittenhouse, Frenchtown.	
L. D. Hagaman, Esq. Frenchtown.		William C. Kline, Frenchtown.	
Mrs. W. Silverthorn, Frenchtown.		E. E. Culver, Frenchtown.	
A. P. Williams, Frenchtown.		Judson Hoff, Frenchtown.	
N. R. Shuster, Everittstown.		Sylvester B. Horner, Frenchtown.	
M. Rittenhouse, Everittstown.		Harriet Barcroft, Frenchtown.	
Mrs. J. F. Case, Everittstown.		Mrs. Hugh Eichlen, Frenchtown.	
William J. Conklin, Frenchtown.		Rev. W. E. Blakeslee, Elizabeth.	
Ida May Conklin, Frenchtown.		Wm. Vanhorn, Idell.	
Mrs. C. A. Slack, Frenchtown.		I. L. Niece, Frenchtown.	
P. M. Mechling, Esq., Pittstown.		Mary A. Stout, Frenchtown.	

NAME.	ADDRESS.
C. A. Wannamaker,	Frenchtown.
Amy Stout,	Frenchtown.
Lavina Pittenger,	Frenchtown.
Rev. W. McCain,	Clinton.
Rev. W. Chamberlin,	Derby, Conn.
J. R. Burgstresser,	Frenchtown.
Bateman Stout,	Everittstown.
Rev. F. Tomlinson,	Quakertown.
Rev. I. N. Vansant,	Bloomsbury.
Joseph M. Pickel,	Pittstown.
Rev. C. Clark, Jr.,	Rockaway.
Mary C. Swan,	Frenchtown.
H. W. Bellis,	Frenchtown.
J. Slater Case,	Trenton.
Anna R. Wright,	Frenchtown.
Mary Tettemer,	Frenchtown.
Minnie Silverthorn,	Frenchtown.
Eli Swallow,	Riegelsville, Pa.
Rev. C. S. Ryman,	Westfield.
Lizzie R. Maxwell,	Frenchtown.
Mrs. Wm. R. Shurtz,	Frenchtown.
Mrs. D. M. Everitt,	Frenchtown.
George W. Eddy,	Frenchtown.
Rev. W. H. Filson,	Frenchtown.
W. O. Roberson,	Frenchtown.
Marinda Henry,	Cherryville.
Joseph Aller,	Frenchtown.
S. R. Dalrymple,	Frenchtown.
Amy T. Pittenger,	Trenton.
Charles S. Maxwell,	Frenchtown.
William Niece,	Frenchtown.
John Butler,	Everittstown.
Edward Lair,	Frenchtown.
Hon. G. O. Vanderbilt,	Princeton.
W. B. Stout,	Philadelphia.
Aaron H. Slack.	Frenchtown.
Esther Salter,	Flemington.
Richard C. Rounsaville,	Chicago.
E. R. Hartpence,	Frenchtown.
Mrs. Mary Godown,	Elwyn, Pa.
C. A. Butterfoss,	Barbertown.

NAME.	ADDRESS.
Emma R. Eckel,	Washington.
Samuel Hoff,	Everittstown.
Mrs. Stacy B. Niece,	Frenchtown.
Andrew K. Kinney,	Frenchtown.
Samuel L. Heller,	Frenchtown.
Mrs. H. F. Gruver,	Uhlertown, Pa.
James Williams,	Erwinna, Pa.
S. A. Eisenhart,	Erwinna, Pa.
Barzila Williams,	Erwinna, Pa.
Mary C. Pittenger,	Frenchtown.
Ezra D. Lennard,	Everittstown.
Mrs. Jane Able,	Frenchtown.
Rev. N. J. Wright,	Long Branch.
Mrs. M. E. Bissey,	Frenchtown.
Theodore Sinclair,	Frenchtown.
Peter C. Mechling,	Frenchtown.
Mrs. N. J. Tomer,	Frenchtown.
Mary E. Opdyke,	Frenchtown.
John R. Salter,	Frenchtown.
Laura Bonham,	Frenchtown.
Alice Schaible,	Uhlertown, Pa.
Alida Apgar,	Finesville.
Mary J. Little	Pittstown.
Samuel H. Stahler,	Frenchtown.
Mrs. G. F. Bloom,	Frenchtown.
Mrs. M. Silverthorn,	Everittstown.
Mrs. Kate Hewitt,	Frenchtown.
B. Newton Curtis,	Lambertville.
Mrs. Henry Hardon,	Frenchtown.
Samuel Dalrymple,	Everittstown.
Mrs. M. S. Morrel,	La Casita, Cal.
Rev. Joseph Gaskill,	Trenton.
Rev. A. M. Palmer,	Newark.
John V. Gordon,	Greensburg, Ia.
Laura Woolverton,	Frenchtown.
Nellie M. Rittenhouse,	Frencht'n.
Mrs. H. I. Srope,	Frenchtown.
Lizzie Stout,	Frenchtown.
L. M. Davis,	Washington.
Jessie Hummer,	Frenchtown.
Anna L. Fritts,	Frenchtown.

NAME.	ADDRESS.	NAME.	ADDRESS.
Mrs. M. Roberson, Frenchtown.		Mrs. M. A. Holcombe, Frencht'n.	
Wilson Roberson, Frenchtown.		John R. Hardon, Frenchtown.	
Mrs. P. R. Hampton, Hainesville.		Mrs. E. H. Wright, Frenchtown.	
Mrs. H. Eilenberg, Frenchtown.		Mrs. Ella Curtis, Everittstown.	
Mrs. Martha Miers, Clinton.		Wilson Lear, Esq., Erwinna.	
C. W. H. Dedrick, Hackettstown.		Mary A. Martin, Mt. Pleasant.	
William Gordon, Frenchtown.		Josie Plum, Frenchtown.	
Britton Pinkerton, Frenchtown.		Anna S. Warford, Frenchtown.	
William V. Gordon, Bethlehem.		E. R. Case, Frenchtown.	
Kate Taylor, Stanhope.		N. D. Smith, Frenchtown.	
A. P. Kachline, Frenchtown.		C. N. Reading, Jr., Frenchtown.	
William Hoff, Frenchtown.		Samuel Rockafellow, Frenchtown.	
Levi M. Hoffman, Frenchtown.		Joseph P. Wilson, Everittstown.	
Armandah Srope, Frenchtown.		Joseph Everitt, Pittstown.	
Anna A. Lyons, Frenchtown.		E. H. Vanderbilt, Easton, Pa.	
Mrs. Frances Kugler, Frenchtown.		Jesse Sinclair, Esq., Riegelsville.	
R. H. Woolverton, Frenchtown.		Lavinia Slack, Frenchtown.	
Mary Bidleman, Camden.		George M. Bidleman, Camden.	
Clara P. Barts, Philadelphia, Pa.